DINING OUT *with* HISTORY

DINING OUT *with* HISTORY

AT ATLANTIC CANADA'S HISTORIC SITES

Jan Feduck

Fitzhenry & Whiteside Limited

Published in Canada by Fitzhenry & Whiteside Limited
209 Wicksteed Avenue, Unit 51, Toronto, ON M4G 0B1

Published in the United States by Fitzhenry & Whiteside Limited
60 Leo M Birmingham Pkwy, Ste 107, Brighton, MA 02135

Fitzhenry & Whiteside acknowledges with thanks the Canada Council for the Arts and the Ontario Arts Council for their support of our publishing program. We acknowledge the financial support of the Government of Canada through the Canada Book Fund (CBF) for our publishing activities.

Library and Archives Canada Cataloguing in Publication

Title: Dining out with history : at Atlantic Canada's historic sites / Jan Feduck.
Names: Feduck, Jan, author.
Description: Paperback edition. | Previously published by the author in 2022. | Includes index.
Identifiers: Canadiana 20230495133 | ISBN 9781554556274 (softcover)
Subjects: LCSH: Cooking—Atlantic Provinces—History. | LCSH: Food—Social aspects—Atlantic Provinces—History. | LCSH: Food habits—Atlantic Provinces—History. | LCSH: Historic sites—Atlantic Provinces—Guidebooks. | LCSH: Atlantic Provinces—Guidebooks. | LCGFT: Guidebooks.
Classification: LCC GT2853.C3 F43 2024 | DDC 394.1/209715—dc23

Publisher Cataloging-in-Publication Data (U.S.)

Names: Feduck, Jan, author.
Title: Dining Out With History : At Atlantic Canada's Historic Sites / Jan Feduck.
Description: Toronto, Ontario : Fitzhenry & Whiteside, 2024. | Includes maps and index. | Summary: "Twenty living history sites that offer us a taste of the past in Nova Scotia, Prince Edward Island, New Brunswick, Newfoundland and Labrador" - Provided by publisher.
Identifiers: ISBN 978-1-55455-627-4 (paperback)
Subjects: LCSH: Atlantic provinces - Guidebooks. | Atlantic provinces - History. | Atlantic provinces - Description and travel. | BISAC: TRAVEL / Canada / Northern Territories / (NB, NL, NS, PE).
Classification: LCC F1035.8F438 | DDC 917.15 - dc23

Design by Andrew Bagatella

Printed in Canada by Copywell

fitzhenry.ca

This book is dedicated to the Historic Sites of Canada.
I also lovingly dedicate this book to my family with
memories of our many travels together.

TABLE OF CONTENTS

INTRODUCTION

"First we eat, then we do everything else." –MFK Fisher

IT WAS A hot summer day and I stood in front of a blazing fire. I was a guest interpreter working with the other women in the Engineer's kitchen at Fortress Louisbourg on Cape Breton Island. I wiped my hands on the heavy wool apron—part of my authentic 1700s clothing —and continued to knead dough. Curious visitors dropped by to watch and ask about what it was like to cook back in time. We shared our experiences and created a wee bit of time travel magic.

Each summer while living on the East Coast, I visit historic sites which share food traditions, and enjoy *chin wags* with the many knowledgeable and passionate interpreters who become characters from history every day.

This book takes the reader on a road trip to twenty of those historic sites in Nova Scotia, Prince Edward Island, New Brunswick, Newfoundland and Labrador. Many cultures have added their tastes to the Maritime cooking pot. It has evolved to include the inherent knowledge of the indigenous peoples living from the land, along with the tastes brought and shared by Nordic, French, African, Scottish, Irish, British and German immigrants.

Food traditions teach us about the indigenous plants that grew on the land and how they were used; what was hunted, fished and raised; what goods were traded from faraway lands and how cultures shared their recipes with others. Time and history have changed our food customs and yet, many of those early dishes continue to be served on our tables today.

Each chapter tours an historic site, tells a tale and shares a few recipes. The stories bring to life the cooking traditions of various periods, and set them in context; as we can see, food, work and life were inextricably linked. Then, as now, food was a vital part of sustaining community and fellowship. Although the stories are not based on facts, some have scatterings of truths woven into the words. Recipes from Eel soup to Flummies offer a chance to cook from the period.

"First we eat,
then we do
everything else."
MFK Fisher
QUÉBEC
Village
Historique
Acadien
Grindstone
Island
NEW
BRUNSWICK
PRINCE EDWARD
ISLAND
Orwell Corner
Historic Village
Jean Pierre
Roma
King's
Landing
Highland Villa
Museum
Balmoral
Grist Mill
UNITED STATES
NOVA SCOTIA
Sherbrook
Village
Ross Farm
Museum
Africville
Museum
Port Royal
Memory Lane
Heritage
Village
Bluenose II
Le Village
Historique Acadien
de la Nouvelle-Écosse
Ross Thomson
House and
Store

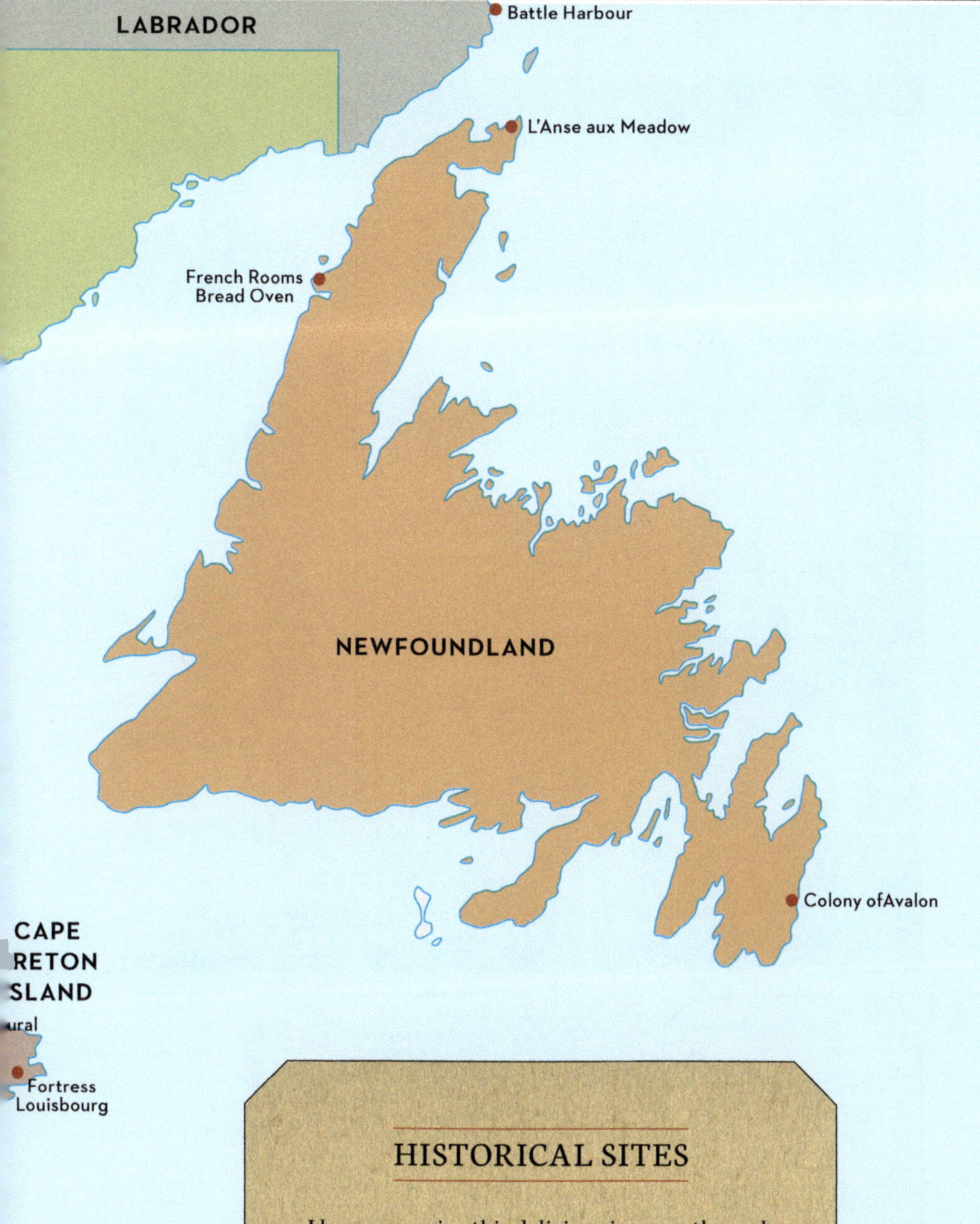

HISTORICAL SITES

I hope you enjoy this delicious journey through the tastes of our past; why not settle in at the table, and dine out with history?

CAPE
BRETON
ISLAND

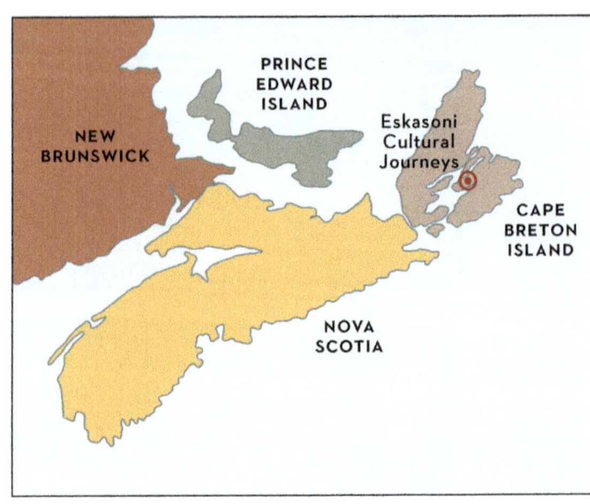
PRINCE
EDWARD
ISLAND
NEW
BRUNSWICK
Eskasoni
Cultural
Journeys
CAPE
BRETON
ISLAND
NOVA
SCOTIA

1 GOAT ISLAND TRAIL
ESKASONI, NS

CHAPTER 1

CAPE BRETON ISLAND

ESKASONI CULTURAL JOURNEYS

The First on This Land

Pjila'si (WELCOME, COME IN and sit down), suggests the sign greeting visitors to Goat Island on the shoreline close to Bras d'Or Lake.

Eskasoni is the largest Mi'kmaq community and was declared a reserve in 1832. It is a growing, prospering community with a strong sense of cultural pride.

Eskasoni Cultural Journeys has created an experience inviting visitors to travel into the past of the Eskasoni peoples, who were the first to live in that area for many centuries before the Europeans arrived.

A guided tour takes guests on a winding two and-a-half kilometre path through the forests that have for time everlasting been home to the Eskasoni. In clearings along the walk, visitors are greeted by Eskasoni interpreters who offer demonstrations and talks to show different aspects of how their people lived in the past.

Matt, one of the guides, leads visitors down the path dressed in a soft deerskin tunic ornately painted with symbols of his culture. Matt is a gifted storyteller who stops often to share a tale or point out a medicinal plant. He shares with passion his deep knowledge and appreciation of his cultural roots.

At one clearing in the forest, visitors learn about and participate in a smudging ceremony, to experience the spirituality of this purifying tradition. Sweetgrass is lit and passed around to each person.

In another clearing is a display of the fishing and hunting tools that were used to provide food prior to the arrival of the Europeans. Each tool is explained along with traditions such as the unique long-handled forks used to fish for eels. Reverence for nature is evident in the fishing and hunting practice of taking only what was needed from the land and water, and using all of it.

A partially built rounded longhouse demonstrates how a warm abode could be made from materials provided by nature. Flexible branches form the frame and bark is placed over the frame.

In a clearing by a lake, visitors experience the power of the drumbeat and the importance of dance, as they are invited to participate.

Still further along the path, a campfire is burning where guests make and eat *Four Cents Bread*, a simple and quick bread. Flour, salt, baking powder and water are mixed together and kneaded into a roll. It is then wrapped around a stick, baked over the fire and enjoyed dipped in molasses with a cup of tea.

Around a table at another stop, the techniques of basketry are taught; visitors learn to weave reeds into a bookmark to take home as a reminder of an extraordinary experience.

Eskasoni Cultural Journeys gives all who visit a deeper understanding and appreciation of how the Eskasoni peoples once lived, as shared through the stories and experiences of those who live now. In all they do, their love and respect for the land, water, and their culture endures.

The Mi'kmaq communities living on the Bras d'Or Lake of Cape Breton Island have hunted eel as a food source for centuries. Eel is cooked in soups, stews or roasted and is now considered a delicacy. Eel has always been fished with respect.

BELOW: Sugar, an interpreter, cooks eel stew.

FISHING MY FIRST EEL

by Shelley Denny

I REMEMBER THE FIRST time I went eel spearing. It was a calm summer evening and the water was so still. I climbed into the boat without my shoes and my pants rolled up. It was late, 11:30 p.m., so I was trying to be quiet as we pushed the boat out from the shore with the light attached to the bow of the boat. A kind man and a friend of a friend took along one other person, and off we went.

Pushing the boat with the eel spear, I was reminded of how to look for eels. "Look for something like smaller logs but with a shadow." As I pushed from the back of the boat, we were quiet, searching. And then I saw one. Without thinking I thrust the spear and held it down to the sand, reminded again not to lift the spear just yet. The eel must wrap itself around the spear before I could bring it into the boat. The eel must give itself to me. All I could feel was the strength of the eel through the spear. I had to keep both hands on the spear. I couldn't lose my first eel!

Doing as I was instructed, I held on until I saw the eel wrap itself around the base of the spear. I brought it up quickly and got it into the boat. I was so proud of myself, yet humbled by the eel's strength and offering - like it transferred its spirit to me through the spear. I knew then what Mi'kmaw responsibility was. And then I did it again.

I saw the second eel and thrusted the spear. "I think you missed," my friend said. "No, I got it." Again, I waited. Not long but it felt like forever before the eel let me bring it in.

What an amazing experience. I was so honoured to spear eels as my ancestors did and as my people continue to do. That night, I thanked the eels and Creator for that honour.

Shelley Denny holds a PhD in Fisheries Governance and shares her first eel fishing experience.

FOUR CENTS BREAD

Courtesy of Eskasoni Cultural Journeys - Our Favourite Recipes

- 2 cups flour
- 2 Tbsp baking powder
- Water,as needed to make a dough texture

THIS BREAD COULD be cooked by forming the dough into a disc shape and cooking over the fire on a metal sheet or by wrapping it around a stick and cooking it directly over the fire.

The ingredients in this bread are common to simple bread made the world over. For our First Nations peoples, this bread could be made in their village, or as they hunted and travelled.

EEL STEW

- Eel
- Water
- Salt and Pepper
- Onion
- Dumplings
- 1 cup flour

BOIL WATER WITH some salt. Chop onion and cook in water.

Then add eel, potatoes, salt and pepper.

Cook until tender and add dumplings.

Add salt and pepper to flour and add water to mix until it forms a firm ball.

Add to eel stew,cover and cook for 20 minutes.

PORT
ROYAL,
NOVA
SCOTIA

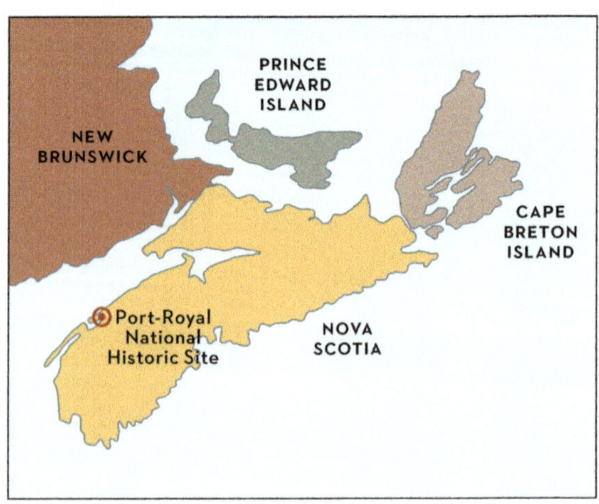
PRINCE
EDWARD
ISLAND
NEW
BRUNSWICK
CAPE
BRETON
ISLAND
Port-Royal
National
Historic Site
NOVA
SCOTIA

53 HISTORIC LANE
GRANVILLE FERRY, NS

CHAPTER 2

PORT ROYAL, NOVA SCOTIA

PORT-ROYAL NATIONAL HISTORIC SITE

With a lesson of Good Cheer

IN 1605 SAMUEL de Champlain excitedly reported to France his belief that "this place was the most pleasant and most suitable for a settlement that we had seen." A recreated Port-Royal now stands on that original site in Nova Scotia, making it possible to travel back to 1605 and envision how the small group of colonists lived in a new land.

Using Champlain's drawings of the fort settlement, a reconstruction was carefully built on the original site, close to the village of Annapolis Royal.

The story begins in 1607 when a nobleman, Pierre Duga arranged with the king to start a settlement called Acadia, to give the French a presence in coastal New England, now Nova Scotia. In return for furs and the religious conversion of the Indigenous population, the king agreed to the expedition. After an unsuccessful attempt on St. Croix, where many lives were lost, the settlement was moved to the Port-Royal site and a habitation was re-built, after the French style of a fortified farm hamlet. The local Mi'kmaq were welcoming to colonists in this area, and proved to be helpful in their survival. They were well respected by the French.

Port-Royal is remembered as an early settlement whose leadership learned to adapt to adversity; one method was by establishing the Order of Good Cheer. This consisted of a group of the noblemen of the settlement who agreed to take turns acting as chief steward, arranging a series of weekly feasts from November to March throughout the winter of 1606. For several days the ruler of the feast would hunt, fish and collect the food for his feast, often with the help of the local Mi'kmaq. According to written reports back to France, settlers hunted moose, caribou, beaver, otter, bear, raccoon and wildcat. They also enjoyed geese, partridge, mallards and other birds, as well as vegetables such as spinach and Jerusalem artichokes. Fish and shellfish such as mussels were used as many of the men had come from fishing areas of France. They made use of herbs and spices to improve the taste of their dishes. Bread was a staple and was baked in the ovens. Desserts such as pear and apple pie as well as marzipan tarts are reported. The cook was kept busy preparing this food for the feasts.

The dining room in present day Port-Royal reflects an air of colonial elegance, and with some imagination visitors can see the procession of men of the Order entering the room to joyous music, carrying platters of food and placing them on the large wooden table. Twenty or thirty from the local Mi'kmaq village attended and sat on the floor around the room. Local chiefs were seated at the table with the dignitaries and treated as equals. All who lived at Port-Royal were served from the head table. These cheerful feasts lifted the spirits of the men that winter and the attention to good nutrition contributed to their health. The settlement existed for some years but was burned by English forces in 1613 after orders to expel the French from the territory. Those who lived in Port-Royal and the area stayed to farm or moved to different areas.

In 1961, Port-Royal was the first historic site in Canada to be reconstructed, and the French government contributed authentic period furniture to add to the ambiance of the site.

Now, visitors can tour Port-Royal to see how the commoners lived as well as the noblemen. A well-furnished kitchen gives a glimpse of where the feasts were prepared and the dining room reveals the heart of what helped the men flourish in their new land that winter of 1606. The smells and tastes must be imagined but the site is a reminder that the French flair for cuisine existed even in the harshest of times, especially with the help of those who had inhabited the lands forever.

FRIENDSHIP AND GOOD FOOD IN HARD TIMES

Port-Royal -Winter of 1605

IN TWO DAYS it would be my honour to feed my friends at Port-Royal at the feast we call The Order of Good Cheer. The icy water burned my hands that day as I tore the mussels away from the slippery rocks. For I would surprise everyone at this week's feast with an Eclade de Moules. My father loved this celebration back in our town by the ocean in France, and now I would bring the custom to the new lands.

I remember my father stood the mussels on a piece of wood, in the sand, in the shape of a cross. Leaning them together, he would cover them with pine needles and light them on fire. Oh the aroma, oh the taste of pine. The Order of Good Cheer would now know what a fine experience could come from the humble shellfish of the seas beside Port-Royal.

Two days ago I was brushing away the snow to collect pine needles. A young hunter from the closest Mi'kmaq settlement came to watch, looking very puzzled. I motioned for him to help me, for I had much food gathering and hunting to do in the next two days. Perhaps he would help me hunt. The next day he proved himself when he killed a deer with one arrow. Together we pulled the deer back to his camp. We hung and skinned it and divided the meat. He took some for his people and I hauled the rest back to the cook to prepare. I made sure to invite my new friend and his mother to attend the feast the next night. As I approached the fort, I could smell the aroma of bread being baked from the outdoor ovens. I was sure my feast would be grand.

Finally the day of the feast arrived and the men gathered around my cross made from mussels. I lit the fire, creating a festive atmosphere as the pine needles burned down and the open mussels appeared. They were piled on a platter to add to the other delicacies. Excitement mounted in the kitchen as the cook and I put foods on to platters and the chevaliers lined up ready to carry one specialty each into the feast room.

I entered first, dressed in my best finery, bearing the Order of Good Cheer medallion around my neck and the napkin of honour over my shoulder. The violins played a lively tune as we marched into the candlelit room. The fire was blazing, providing warmth for our Mi'kmaq

friends seated on the floor around the room. The air was festive, and for a time we would forget the problems of daily living. We placed the platter on the main table where Samuel de Champlain, Chief Membertou and the other esteemed members of the Order sat. I noticed the anticipation on the faces of the men at the other tables. I looked around the room for my guest of honour that night. As we handed out bread to our Mi'kmaq friends seated on the edge I spotted my hunting comrade. Taking his hand I pulled him to the table and in his hands I placed some mussels. I crossed my hands over my heart and our eyes forged our friendship.

ÉCLADE DE MOULE (MUSSELS)

Many of the men who inhabited Port-Royal came from a seaside area in western France. When Samuel de Champlain established his Feast of Good Cheer, this was said to be one of the dishes served to remind the men of life at home. Mussels were abundant and there was an air of festivity to this method of preparation.

- Written as a description, this recipe uses amounts at the discretion of the cook.

FIRST THE MUSSELS must be collected from the sea, as well as pine needles from the forest.

Take a piece of wood and hammer four nails in the centre.

Rest the first mussel against the nails hinged side up, and place the remaining mussels in the shape of a cross or a circle, each mussel resting on the others.

Cover with a bed of dried pine needles and light on fire.

When the pine needle fire has burnt out, the mussels will have opened. If not, add more needles.

The pine needles give the mussels a distinctive taste. Below shows the mussels covered in pine needles and set ablaze. When the pine needles burn the mussels are exposed.

CAPE
BRETON
ISLAND

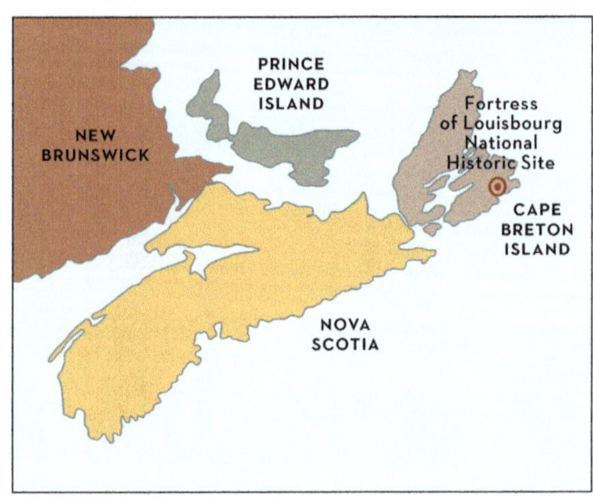
PRINCE
EDWARD
ISLAND
NEW
BRUNSWICK
Fortress
of Louisbourg
National
Historic Site
CAPE
BRETON
ISLAND
NOVA
SCOTIA

259 PARK SERVICE RD.
LOUISBOURG, NS

CHAPTER 3

CAPE BRETON ISLAND

FORTRESS OF LOUISBOURG NATIONAL HISTORIC SITE

A French Fortress and Town

ON A REMOTE spit of land on the coast of Cape Breton Island, a walled town appears faintly, emerging from the fog. Visitors walk a path out past the fishermen's huts, past the cod hanging on racks, and through huge stone gates into the year 1744.

Fortress Louisbourg is alive with activity each summer, as interpretive staff and children attending programs become the fishermen, soldiers, merchants, townsfolk, Mi'kmaw and nobility of the town. The smell of sea air and baking bread surrounds the strolling minstrels and elegantly dressed aristocratic women who pass by, gossiping, on the cobbled streets. It takes little imagination for visitors to be swept up into the lives of those who lived in Louisbourg.

This fortified French town was settled in 1713 and thrived for the next fifty years. Its chief business—fishing and salting cod for trade with markets in Europe and the Caribbean—made it the busiest port in North America. Hundreds of slaves were brought to Fortress Louisbourg. One of them, Marie Marguerite Rose, came as a slave who was eventually freed and ran her own successful inn and tavern; her story is an important part of the history.

In 1760, Fortress Louisbourg was captured by the British and dismantled. Most of its French residents returned to France and the thriving town once again became land beside the ocean. Two hundred years later, unemployed mine workers were recruited to rebuild the Fortress according to historic plans—the largest historic reconstruction project in North America—and it has become an impressive recreation of its former glory.

Now, visitors can peer into kitchens of the past, to watch soldier's bread being baked in the King's Bakery, and buy a loaf to take home and taste. Around the corner, guests can walk through the aromatic gardens to visit the Engineer's kitchen where a chicken is cooking on a mechanical spit jack in an open hearth fireplace; or watch the making of rich hot chocolate, and see white bread and side dishes being prepared for a dinner for the wealthy. The Mi'kmaw Interpretive Centre tells the story of

how the First Nations community helped the French as they settled, and celebrates their strong ongoing relationship.

In two eateries, the Hôtel de la Marine and the Grandchamps Restaurant, visitors order full course meals or à la carte food such as the townsfolk and soldiers would once have eaten. Dishes like pea soup, meat pie, fish and homemade bread use recipes and cooking methods from two hundred and fifty years ago. To deliver the authentic 1740s dining experience, visitors are provided with pewter dishes and a single spoon.

Taverns once lined the cobbled harbour street at Fortress Louisbourg. At a recreated tavern guests can taste and learn about the history of Caribbean rum popular with the sailors and soldiers of the Fortress. Local craft beers are available to remind visitors of brews of the past.

Ghostly fog uncurls around the stone gates when it is time to walk back to the present. The Fortress of Louisbourg experience offers a journey that builds deeper understanding of the lives of some of Nova Scotia's earliest immigrants.

BAKING BREAD AT LOUISBOURG

THERESE CLEARED A small hole in the frost on the window of the garrison bakery. She could see her brother Jacques, faintly lit by the fire, kneading dough in a big wooden trough. In her new position in the Engineer's kitchen in Louisbourg, Therese was learning to make white bread, and she wanted to watch Jacques make Soldier's Bread at the bakery for the garrison.

Therese and her brother had grown up in a fishing family on the outside of the high stone walls of the fortress. Their mother had taught them both to make bread, but now they were in service to others and had to learn new ways. She had seen Jacques hauling huge bags of flour from the ships in the harbour. When she met her brother at the well that morning, he handed her a bite of dense, dark bread.

"Nothing like the bread I make at the Engineer's House," she'd said. "We use only the finest white flour. Oh Jacques, you should feel it. Like silk."

"Only for the rich," Jacques said with a frown. "Don't get used to it.

Here's how we make bread for the soldiers. We start in the night and by morning we turn out one hundred of those round loaves. That's a lot of mixing, and the kneading takes all my strength. The soldiers are allowed one six-pound loaf every four days but they share their loaves so the bread is not

rock-hard. Goes with their soup and bean rations."

Therese picked up her wooden water bucket and headed up the hill, through the gate, across the gardens rich with herbs and into the elegant home of Monsieur Vergery de Verville. Marie Marguerite Rose had come to visit the kitchen. She was amazed by this determined woman, a freed slave and now the owner of an inn and tavern. Well respected in town, she was known to be an excellent cook.

"About time you got back," shouted the head cook. "We won't get this bread made until 1752, if you don't get your hands in that flour."

Therese mixed her dough and kneaded the loaves with care. This was the bread that would be used to make delicate sandwiches served for an upcoming celebration. The cook busied herself making fruit-shaped marzipan sweets, a treat so special that Marie could only dream of a taste.

When she met Jacques at the well the next day, she pulled a small white piece of bread from the pocket of her apron and put it in his rough hand.

"White and soft like a cloud," said Jacques. "Don't ever share it with a soldier."

A soldier in the bakery holds a loaf of soldier's bread from the oven. Each soldier was rationed one six-pound loaf each four days along with salt meat and dried vegetables.

FORTRESS OF LOUISBOURG

18TH CENTURY FRENCH SOLDIER'S BREAD

Recipes from Fortress Louisbourg (Courtesy of Parks Canada). This recipe is available online through the Parks Canada Heritage Gourmet.

- ½ Tbsp (8g) dry yeast
- 1½ cups (359 ml) lukewarm water
- ½ Tbsp (4g) salt
- 3 cups (750ml/400g) stone-ground whole-wheat flour
- 1 cup (250 ml/130g) stone-ground rye flour

FOLLOW THE YEAST package directions to get started. Mix in a large bowl: the yeast preparation, any remaining water and one third of the flour. Beat for at least 100 strokes.

Cover and let rise for ½ hour.

Beat down and fold in the salt. Add the remaining flour 1 cup at a time until a workable dough forms that is not too stiff. Turn out onto a floured surface and lightly knead until smooth, about 5 or 6 minutes, adding flour as required to prevent sticking.

Place in greased bowl, cover and let rise in a warm place until double in bulk. Depending on the weather, this could take between 4 and 12 hours.

Punch down, let rise again until double in bulk. (A second rising improves the texture and taste. This step may be skipped.) Punch down and turn dough out on floured surface and knead slightly.

Divide dough into 2 equal portions and shape into rounds. Let these rise until the surface of the dough yields to the touch, about half an hour.

Place on greased baking sheets and bake in an oven preheated to 400°F (200°C) for 25 -30 minutes.

FORTRESS OF LOUISBOURG

WHITE BREAD

White bread was made using refined flour and was only eaten by the wealthy and upper-class citizens of Fortress Louisbourg.

- 6 cups lukewarm water
- 1 rounded Tbsp dry yeast
- 1½ Tbsp sugar
- 1½ Tbsp salt
- 1½ Tbsp vegetable oil
- 16 - 18 cups white all-purpose flour, stone-ground whole-wheat flour

1. In a large bowl soften yeast with 2 cups warm water. When yeast is foamy, add the remaining 4 cups of warm water with the salt, sugar and oil and mix well. Then add 8 cups of flour and beat well until batter is smooth and small bubbles form. Cover bowl and place in a warm place for 2 hours.
2. Beat mixture vigorously. Then add flour one cup at a time until a workable dough forms (not too stiff). Turn out on floured surface and knead gently until smooth (3 or 4 minutes). Add flour as required to prevent sticking.
3. Place in greased bowl. Cover and let rise in a warm place until doubled in bulk.
4. Punch down and turn dough out on floured surface and knead slightly. Divide dough into 4 equal portions and shape into rounds. Place on a greased cookie sheet and let rise in a warm place (cover with a cloth) until almost doubled in bulk.
5. Bake in a pre-heated oven at 425°F. for 15 minutes. Reduce heat to 350°F and continue to bake for another 25 to 30 minutes, or until loaves are lightly brown on top and sound hollow when tapped.
6. Remove from pans and place on racks until cool.

MODERN TIPS

- Warm the flour in the oven so that the rising is not slowed by the addition of cold flour.
- Brush tops of baked loaves with oil or butter if you prefer a less crusty loaf.
- In step 4, do not let your loaves rise too long or you will have bread that is full of holes.

91 OLD CHURCH RD.
LOWER WEST PUBNICO, NS

CHAPTER 4

LOWER WEST PUBNICO, NOVA SCOTIA

LE VILLAGE HISTORIQUE ACADIEN

An Acadien Fishing Settlement comes alive

THE SMELL OF pie baking in the oven dances across the senses of visitors who enter Le Village Historique Acadien, for the Acadians are known for their pie.

The dirt trail in the seventeen-acre village slopes down to the fishing dock and looks across the harbour to East Pubnico. Here, visitors are invited into the homes and families of a settlement in southern Nova Scotia. Settled originally in 1653 by Sieur Phillipe Mius d'Entremont, and still inhabited by Acadian families, this is the oldest Acadian area populated by its founder's descendants. Two authentic homes, a fishing and boat building shed, post office, blacksmith shop, lighthouse and barns with the vast marshes behind them create a landscape that paints a true picture of life here in the early 1900s.

Inside the Charles Duon House, guests are greeted by the woman of the house and the smell of food cooking in the kitchen's cast iron stove.

"My ancestors lived in this very house," says the woman at the stove, telling her guests about the brown bread, baked beans, and molasses cookies or pies they might have eaten there.

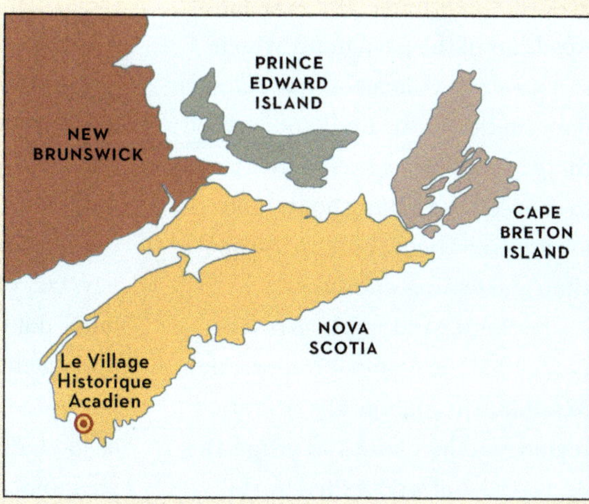

A visit to the d'Entremont House is a chance to meet a second family and tour their home. Dressed like Acadians of the past, many who tell stories at the village today are descendants of those who lived and worked these lands years ago. They are proud to show off the fishing boats, nets and lobster traps being built in the boat shop and fishing shanty.

Beginning in 1755, in an event now called the Acadian Deportation, Acadians throughout the Atlantic region had their land and properties destroyed and were exiled by the British. Many families were separated and many perished at sea. In 1764, the British government permitted Acadians to return to British territories. Rather than the fertile land they had once inhabited, they were resettled nearby on rocky lands by the sea, so had to adapt to a fishing lifestyle.

Pyramid-shaped piles of hay or haystacks on platforms called chaffauds dot the marshlands, showcasing the ingenuity of the Acadians who harvested and stored the marsh grass as fodder for their cattle. Chicken and pigs were the main sources of meat,

and cows were raised for dairy products. Clanging from the blacksmith shop draws visitors inside to see what is being created.

Off in the distance is the lighthouse, once on Quoggeniche Island, relocated here to replace a lantern that was held up on a post to warn ships of the rocks.

After visiting the Acadian families of the village, it's time to experience a taste of the past at the Café du Crique. This café is known for people requesting "the last piece of pie."

The cooks explain that those lucky enough to get the last piece of pie get all the extra goodness of the left-over filling from the pie plate. And with this homemade pie, that makes a difference.

Lunch at the café may feature homemade bread and molasses, a bowl of hearty soup and fresh blueberry pie; a real taste of history. The culture of the Acadians in southern Nova Scotia is still very proud and strong. Le Village historique acadien celebrates hardworking ancestors who knew how to eat and live well.

THE LAST PIECE OF PIE

Pubnico, Nova Scotia, Autumn 1905

MÉMÈRE D'ENTREMONT SAT in her rocker knitting and trying to decide what to put in her pie for dinner tonight. Then she had an idea she knew would keep her grandchildren busy and give her a peaceful day.

"My petit chers," she said to the little ones who were sitting by the stove. "Let's surprise Maman and Papa with their favourite pie tonight. But I am too old to run around the land for the makings so I will make a deal with you. The first person to arrive with a bowl of cranberries will get the 'last piece of pie'."

"But cranberries are not for pie," said Danielle.

"Oh, but you just wait and see," replied Mémère.

The children knew what this magic term, "the last piece of pie," meant and they ran off with their baskets.

It was a haying day and Henri and Paulette were busy making salt haystacks in the marsh to provide extra feed for the cattle. Mémère knew they would be too tired to cook for the family after a day in the fields. So her wrinkled hands put down their knitting. She had planned favots au lard (pork and beans), homemade bread and their favourite pie.

The beans had soaked overnight and Mémère d'Entremont climbed up into the cupboard and brought down the much-loved pottery crock for beans. It had been in the family for generations. She went to the shed where the pork was smoked and salted for winter, to get a piece for the beans. Cutting the tough meat into slices, she put a layer on the bottom of the bean crock. Layering the soaked beans and the salt pork, she filled the crock to the top and put it in the oven, adding some wood to the fire. It would cook all day. Yesterday Mémère had baked bread from molasses, flour and oatmeal, and that would be perfect with the beans.

Across the field, Danielle pulled the cranberries from the bushes as fast as she could. She noticed that her brother had wandered off and was digging worms. She was sure she would earn that "last piece of pie."

As Mémère mixed the ingredients for her pie crust she looked out the window and across the marsh. This was the final day of building haystacks. Two days ago, they had cut the marsh grass and raked it into les grands rouleaux. The platforms had been built, and today the workers would throw the hay to the worker atop the platforms to build into a pyramid shape. This would keep the marsh hay above the tides. Mémère could remember her grandfather building the haystacks the same way, all those years ago.

The door banged open and in ran Danielle, almost spilling her bowl overflowing with cranberries. Mémère cooked them with raisins. From memory and with well-trained hands, she added just the right amount of sugar, flour and spices, cinnamon and nutmeg.

Little Pierre made his way through the door proudly holding up his worms, knowing that he would not have "the last piece of pie" that night but that he could still scare his sister.

That night, the family said their blessings at the table after a long day in the fields. The bean crock was set on the table beside the loaf of bread and butter. Tired faces lit up when the (Mock) Cherry pie was set on the table.

"So that's where my cranberries are hidden," whispered Danielle to her grandmother.

"And the last and best piece of pie is for Danielle," said Mémère, as she heaped all the remaining fruit and juice from the pie plate on top of her piece.

OVAL

RECIPE FOR MOCK CHERRY PIE

Courtesy of the Village historique acadien de la Nouvelle-Écosse

- 1 Tbsp flour dissolved
- ½ cup water
- 1 tsp vanilla
- 1 cup cranberries
- 1 cup sugar
- 1 egg

Mix flour with sugar and stir.

Add water, egg and vanilla. Whisk together.

Add the cranberries.

Put in a lattice crust pie and bake for 35 minutes in a 400°F oven.

Submitted by Roseline Le Blanc from her Maman, Corinne et Grand-mère.

9 CHARLOTTE LANE
SHELBURNE, NS

CHAPTER 5

SHELBURNE, NOVA SCOTIA

ROSS-THOMSON HOUSE AND STORE MUSEUM

A Seaside Shipping and Trading Centre

TO WALK THE streets of the historic section of the village of Shelburne, Nova Scotia is to take a walk back to the 1700's. Many buildings remain from the day they were built and hydro wires have been buried adding to the authenticity. This community grew around the well- situated harbour, first named Port Roseway and later Shelburne, to honour a Lord. Ships headed north from America with four hundred Empire Loyalists who were escaping the turmoil of the American Revolution. They were promised free land, tools, and provisions in return for loyalty to the British King George. With them, travelled the freed slaves that became the first Black Empire Loyalists, who also settled close to this area. The town grew to a population of ten thousand and became the fourth largest community in North America.

Eventually many settlers moved away when the promises of land and provisions could not be kept for such a large number of arrivals.

A tall, brown- shingled building remains on a quiet side street where it was built by George and Robert Ross in 1785. The Ross Thomson House gives us an authentic glimpse

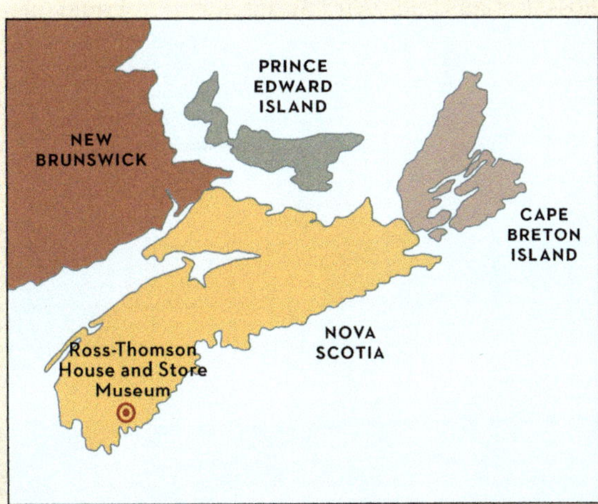

into the lives of commercial enterprise and trading when the town was thriving. The Ross brothers were international traders and sent ships between Europe, the Caribbean and up the coast of America. They traded pickled herring for salt from the Turks Islands, tobacco from the Carolinas and Virginia, flour from New England, rum, molasses and sugar from the West Indies as well as port and wine from Madeira.

Entering through the front wooden door, the visitor walks into the storeroom past stacks of bales and mysterious parts for sailing ships. A large wooden barrel from 1760 that held 1100 pints of port remains. It travelled by ship from Porto, Portugal to give townsfolk a taste of fine liquor.

Shelves of dry goods behind the counter are mixed with arts and crafts for sale, reminiscent of the past.

This building housed the shop, storage room and also a home for the Ross brothers and their families for many years. In the storeroom, the woman of the house shows how a coil of tobacco was cut off and sold by the inch for men to smoke in their clay pipes. She will happily show off her well-planned garden. After picking a basket of chive blossoms, she gives the visitors a handwritten recipe for chive vinegar that she wrote with a quill pen. The passionate historical interpreter likes to have a cooking project happening and loves to share her tastes through her recipe collection. A tour through the living quarters of the building surprises the visitor with colourful walls and elegant furnishings of the past.

Over the years this building has been used as a shop, storage facility for traded goods, post office, home and even a militia-gathering place during the Fenian raids.

This meticulously preserved building is alive with history and stories of the past. "If only those walls could talk."

SWEET·CICELY

WAITING FOR THE SHIPS

Ross Thompson House, Shelburne, Nova Scotia 1795

DORCAS WAS PICKING chives from the garden outside the house and trading post that she and her husband Robert ran in Shelburne. She would use the blossoms to make vinegar. She stuffed the blossoms into the jars and filled them with vinegar that had been heated over the fire.

Placing the warm jars on the wooden sideboard she sat down to look out the window. It was one of those hot summer days that felt heavy with dampness. The clock ticked slowly it seemed until the time when Robert would return home from his trading trip to the Caribbean.

She heard the door of the shop slam shut and left the living quarters to help the customer. She didn't recognize the woman, but knew she must be visiting town from the neighboring community of Birchtown where the Black Loyalists had established a colony.

"Do you have any vinegar?" asked the woman.

"I do, and what would you be making?" Dorcas replied.

"An old drink that my grandma from the islands taught me: Switchel. It's for the farmers in the fields on hot days."

"Please share with me how you make this refreshing drink. What is your name?" said Dorcas while she looked for her quill pen and a piece of paper to note the receipt.

"My name is Nellie and my grandma told me this; take some water and add half as much cider vinegar. Add a few spoonfuls of molasses, maybe a bit of honey, and then grate some ginger into the mix. Pour it into a crock and you have a refreshing drink for them working in the fields."

"Thanks for sharing . . . and here, take a jar of my chive vinegar, no charge. Come back again."

Just at that moment, Dorcas's son ran through the door screaming that his father's ship had come into the harbour.

A shiver of relief ran through Dorcas, for when Robert left on each trading trip, she feared the seas would take him away forever. But again, he had returned. Now the shelves in the store would be full again. There would be flour from New England for the townsfolk to make bread, and molasses and sugar from the West Indies for making sweets and tobacco for the men to put in their pipes and smoke. The store would be bustling again with those eager to buy the latest goods and she would not hear the clock ticking, for she would be so busy.

She ran down to the harbour, dodging the men carrying barrels of molasses and bundles of goods. She could see Robert on the deck, giving orders and looking proud for he was a hero when he returned. She turned back towards home to make her husband a special dinner that would taste unforgettable after weeks on the seas.

This story is a work of fiction and does not correspond to actual dates, events or individuals at Ross-Thomson House and Store Museum.

CHIVE BLOSSOM VINEGAR

- Fresh Chives with blossoms

HARVEST THE BLOSSOMS from the chives. Soak them in clear, cold water.

Drain and pat dry.

Heat white vinegar over a slow flame until quite warm, but not boiling.

Place blossoms in jar. Top with heated vinegar. Set in a dark place for two weeks.

Strain and enjoy the beautiful pink dressing.

SWITCHEL

This refreshing drink was called haymakers punch and was used widely as a refreshing and healthy drink for those working in the fields. It is said to have originated in the Caribbean and much trading was done in that part of the world in the 18th century. It also served as a rum substitute on British Navy ships. Here is the recipe given to me by interpretive staff at the Ross Thomson House, although there are many different ways to make this beverage.

- 8 cups water
- 1 cup brown sugar
- ¾ cup cider vinegar
- ½ cup molasses
- ½ tsp ground ginger

MIX ALL INGREDIENTS over low heat until sugar dissolves. Let cool and serve warm, diluted with water.

School
Section 60

4119 HIGHWAY 223
IONA, NS

CHAPTER 6

CAPE BRETON ISLAND

HIGHLAND VILLAGE, BAILE NAN GÀIDHEAD

A Bit of Scotland

THE VIEW AFTER a climb up the hill at the Highland Village overlooks the Barra Strait of the Bras d'Or Lakes and with no stretch of the imagination, one could be in Scotland, or back in time on Cape Breton Island.

The Highland Village in Iona, Cape Breton Island, Nova Scotia gives visitors a sense of how life was for the Gaelic immigrants who arrived from the Scottish Highlands between1770 and 1840. These newcomers left their homeland for a new life free of the high property rents and demands of their English landlords.

A collection of twelve buildings has been preserved by moving or reconstruction, demonstrating four eras in Gaelic Nova Scotia from 1770 to the 1920s.

The journey begins with a visit to a Herbridean-style Blackhouse to hear stories of Gaels preparing to leave Scotland. Guests move through time to the more comfortable wooden farm homes that the immigrants eventually built. In the barns and fields farm animals graze, and the sound of the clanging of the hammer leads to a visit with the blacksmith at the forge working to fulfil the needs of his community.

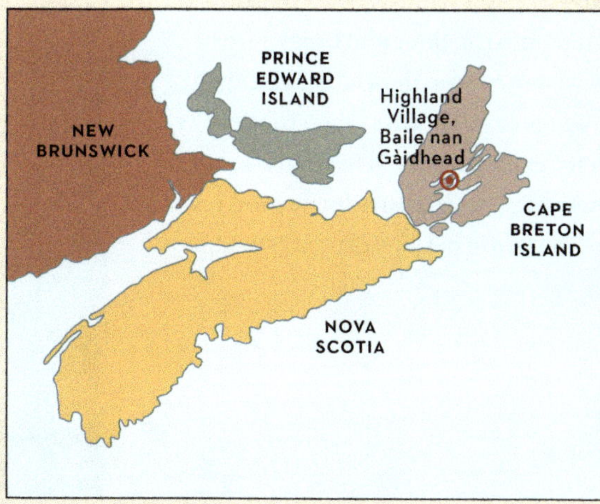

Costumed guides demonstrate the collecting of wool, and the dying and weaving that were used to make blankets and clothing. Women demonstrate quilting, make delicate laces, and hook rugs, showing how they used their skills to beautify their homes.

Visitors can watch how women bake in an open-hearth fireplace. The schoolhouse is as it was when long-ago students attended, and the old general store re-creates the experience of shopping in a different time.

At the top of the hill is the Malagawatch Church. This church was sailed across the Bras d'Or Lake to a new resting place in the Highland Village in 2003. Special musical events occur during the summer by candlelight and continue to bring the spirit of the church alive.

If visitors arrive at the right moment, they might be invited into a kitchen cèilidh at the home atop the hill. A fiddler plays old Gaelic tunes, and a visitor from the past might step onto the floor and break into a barefooted step dance. The Highland Village recalls times when those who left Scotland worked hard to start a new life; their culture is a lasting part of the fabric of Cape Breton Island.

SAMHAINN (HALLOWEEN DAYS)

October 31, 1804, Iona, Cape Breton Island

CORA WIPED HER hands on her apron and looked out over the fields to see if her wee bairn (child) Isla was coming back with turnips from the garden.

Isla trudged across the fields, the sun catching her blond curls, and stopped to eat a raspberry. The fields were rich with foods to be harvested and put down for the winter. Isla followed her mama into the house and Cora kissed her raspberry lips with thanks.

"I ken we'll be havin a fuarag (see recipe) for our gathering this evening," Cora told the children. " It's Samhainn (a Scottish celebration similar to Halloween), and time to have fun and celebrate the harvest. First we'll carve those turnips into faces to scare away bad spirits, and we must make costumes. "

Cora looked through the spider-web-covered window, off into the field, and watched Angus working to bring in the vegetables. The stones in the fields reminded her of her childhood home in the stone hut in Scotland when life was tough. She looked around the wooden home filled with furniture that she and Angus had built. Time and Cape Breton Island had brought her many gifts.

"Sit by the fire, wee bairns, and I'll tell ye what it was like for your seanair and seanmhair (grandpa and grandma). When I was wee, we lived in a stone hut with your great-grandparents. It was on the Isle of Barra, off the coast of Scotland. The wind stung our faces every day up high on the hill, and no trees blocked our view of the ocean waves. Trees had long ago been cut for firewood and we used peat from the bogs to make our fire. Inside the hut was a bare earth floor with a fire in the middle. The smoke stung our eyes, so we only went inside to keep warm. The pot was always boiling and we often had a sore tummy from hunger. Your grandparents rented a small piece of land and we had a few cows, chickens and pigs. There was little to eat and I remember the landlord making me ma cry."

"Your father and I, we came by ship . . . ." she said, and her voice faded out.

"Why did you leave? How did you get here? What did you eat? Where did you sleep?"

"Tha beatha math, wee bairns, just know your life is good," she said. "Now run off and let me prepare the surprise dish for Samhainn, before our friends arrive."

Mysterious people arrived that evening, dressed like funny strangers, and sat in a circle around the edge of the parlour. Angus started the music with his fiddle. Elspeth, from the next farm, started to step dance in the middle of the room. There was laughing and singing and storytelling and Cora felt content. She brought out a big dish of Fuarag and put it in the middle of the room. Inside the mixture of oatmeal, whipped cream and sugar, trinkets were hidden, each one with a special meaning. The person who spooned up a ring could expect to be married, a thimble foretold a destiny as an old maid, a button meant bachelorhood and a coin promised riches. There was lots of laughter and teasing amongst those good friends that night.

One by one, the family awoke the next day to a warm kitchen and fresh bonnach on the table. Cora had wakened early to prepare the special bread for her family.

Each child took the bonnach, stood in front of the mirror and ate a bite.

"You should see your future husband over your shoulder in the mirror," Cora told the little ones.

"I see him," shouted Isla.

Cora made a wish that her children would have the happiness in the future that she and Angus had worked so hard to give them in this new land.

BONNACH

Courtesy of the Highland Village

- 2 cups flour
- 1 cup bran
- 2 tsp baking powder
- 1 tsp salt
- 2 Tbsp sugar
- ¼ cup lard or shortening
- 1 cup milk
- ¼ cup water
- 2 Tbsp sugar

MIX FLOUR, BRAN, BAKING powder and salt together in a bowl.

Mix into the flour mixture the lard (or shortening) milk and water. (More water can be added if mixture seems dry).

Roll out and shape.

Bake at 350°F for 30 minutes.

FUARAG

Courtesy of the Highland Village

To celebrate Samhainn, add a ring to symbolize marriage, a thimble to symbolize an old maid, a button to predict bachelorhood, and a coin to predict wealth. Each person takes a spoonful and if you have an item in your spoon, your future for the next year has been predicted.

- 1 cup rolled oats (toasted oats optional)
- ¾ cup sugar (or to taste)
- 2 cups whipping cream

COMBINE WHIPPING CREAM and sugar in a chilled bowl, and whip together until soft peaks form.

Fold in oats.

Serve topped with brown sugar.

660 MATHESON BROOK RD.
TATAMAGOUCHE, NS

CHAPTER 7

DENMARK, NOVA SCOTIA

BALMORAL GRIST MILL

Where the millstones ground the grain

AFTER A DRIVE on red gravel roads through forests in northern Nova Scotia, the statuesque red Balmoral Grist Mill comes into view, perched beside a gorge on Matheson Brook.

At the Balmoral Grist Mill, farmers' grains became the fine flours and cereals that local families used to bake their Scottish breads and sweets from 1875 until it finally closed in the 1950s. Now, it's up and running again for visitors who can take home a fresh bag of oatmeal for a real taste of the past.

Matheson Brook powered at least six gristmills at a time when there were hundreds in Nova Scotia in the late 1800s. The Balmoral mill hums with the well-timed rhythm of its workings. Hydraulic water turbines were used to run the mill until later years when waterpower gave way to gas and then electricity.

Two families, the MacKays and the MacDonalds, worked the mill in its eighty years of operation. The fathers each passed the mill to their sons. Running the mill required skills in carpentry, mechanics and stonework, a knowledge of the grinding of grains and an ability to manage the business.

Alexander McKay opened the mill in 1874, in what was once a bustling town and community of Scottish settlers. McKay ground wheat flour,

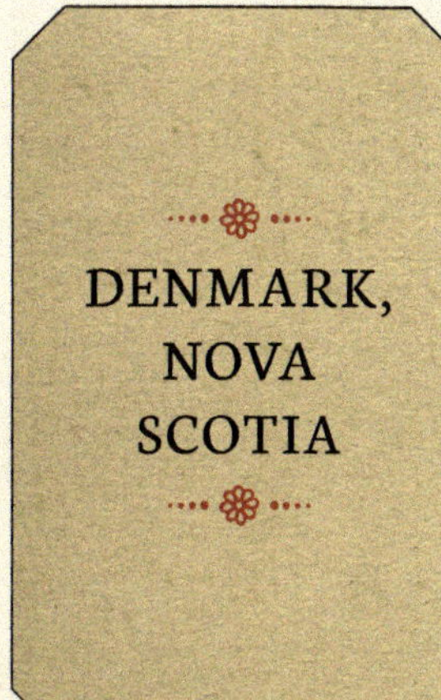

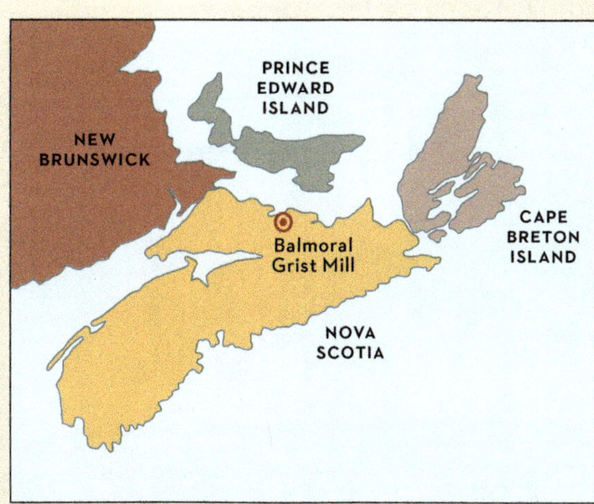

(what we know as white), whole wheat, wheat shorts (for cream of wheat), and bran. He also ground barley, rye, corn and buckwheat. Five pairs of stones were used, including granite and French burrstone, depending on the grain. McKay's tasty oatmeal was in high demand. He dried the oats for six hours on a large metal floor plate over a sugar maple wood fire, giving the oats a fine taste.

The last miller, Archie McDonald, was committed to keeping Balmoral Grist Mill running but was forced to close down in the mid-1950s as commercial flours became readily available and the need for the mill declined. The restoration of the Mill began in the 1960s to create a living history museum, and it opened to the public in 1970. Now, a tour through the mill shows the workings of the many pieces of wooden machinery and belts cleverly crafted to grind different types and grades of grains. At first glance it looks complicated, but the power source makes the big central gear (spur wheel) turn and the top stone connects or disconnects to the spur wheel to make it run. The central gear powers all the belts and elevators. Sifting grains through different types of screens produces different grinds. The aroma of freshly ground grain evokes a time when farmers gathered at the mill, bringing their harvests. They returned home with all the local news and the grains and cereals to feed their families.

Visitors leave the mill with a new appreciation of what it took to create flours and cereals. Bake oatcakes made with grains from Balmoral Grist Mill, and you will have a taste of a cookie with history.

DANCING AND OATCAKES AT THE MILLS

Balmoral Mill, Denmark, Nova Scotia, February 1880

WHEN SHE POKED her head through the heavy wooden door of the Balmoral Grist Mill, Mrs. McKenzie saw a snowstorm of dust. She clung to the china plate of oatcakes with one hand and covered her face with the other as she climbed down the stairs, looking for old man McKay. What she saw stopped her dead in her tracks. Through the snowfall of grain it looked for all the world like the miller was step dancing.

"McKay," she shouted, " I brought your favourite treats."

He stopped his step dancing long enough to take the plate of oatcakes from her cold hands and reached out for her to join him in his dance.

"It's cold, gotta keep warm," he said, letting out a loud cough, and he kept dancing.

"Come on, join in."

Mrs. McKenzie heard no music, but when she listened she understood the secret tunes that gave McKay his beat. It was the quiet rhythm of the huge wooden wheels, cogs, grindstones and the fall of water outside creating a harmony, a good dancing beat. When McKay stopped to take a breath, he listened carefully.

"Shhhhhh!" He motioned with his finger over his mouth.

"Can tell if it's all workin properly by the rhythm," he told her breathlessly.

"Whatever do you mean?" asked Mrs. McKenzie.

"I listen to the Song of the Damsel," he explained. "Each stone makes a different damsel sound when it turns, and that's how I can tell when all is well."

Mrs. McKenzie had never strayed far from her kitchen, but she felt that now she understood the heart and soul of the Mill and also a bit of the heart and soul of McKay.

She took a step forward, and danced over to the secret spot where McKay kept a cloth bag of his best oats for her to take home. She climbed the steep stairs, glancing back to see him still dancing to the rhythm of the machinery through the haze of flour dust.

"Come back real soon," McKay yelled over the noise.

Mrs. McKenzie returned home with a smile on her face. Right away, she began her next batch of oat cakes for old man McKay, for that was her reason to visit the mill. Her husband had passed four years ago and now she had no oats from the farm to be ground. McKay always saved some of the best oats to give her, hiding them in a cloth bag under the tool table. And she loved to see him smile when she visited.

Mrs. McKenzie fired up her woodstove. She sifted the fine quality oats through her fingers, admiring their aroma, and poured two teacups full into a bowl.

These taste better than the oats back in Scotland, she thought. Was it the stone that ground them or how he roasted the oats on the metal floor with just the right wood? Or, more likely, was McKay just a wizard with the grains?

To the oatmeal, she poured in one cup of flour. It was the special snowy white flour that had been sifted through the screens one extra time. Her secret was to add one teacup full of brown sugar along with the other ingredients. She added her own touch to her grandmother's rule that sugar was never to be added to oatcakes back in Scotland. She formed the dough into a ball, and using her rolling pin she made a thick round. With her biscuit cutter, she shaped the small, delicate oat cakes just the way McKay liked them. When she put her hand in the stove, she could tell just the perfect temperature to bake them.

As they baked, she settled into her rocking chair, closed her eyes and pictured old man McKay tucking into her oat cakes. She would go back to the Mill more often now, to dance to the beat of the Song of the Damsel. She liked the sound of that.

BALMORAL OATCAKES

Recipe courtesy of Balmoral Grist Mill

From a collection of recipes by Christene MacDonald (wife of owner and operator of Balmoral Grist Mill from 1940 - 1954. Miller of museum from 1970 - 1979).

- ½ cup margarine
- ½ cup brown sugar
- ½ cup evaporated milk
- 1 cup Balmoral Wheat flour
- ½ cup Balmoral whole wheat flour
- 2½ - 3 cups Balmoral oatmeal
- ¾ tsp baking soda
- ½ tsp salt

IN A MIXING BOWL, blend margarine and brown sugar, mixing well.

Add milk. Stir in flour, soda, salt and whole wheat. Add oatmeal to make mixture stiff enough to handle.

Turn mixture out on floured board, divide into three portions. Roll out thin, trim edges and mark in squares.

Place on ungreased baking sheet and bake 350°F until golden brown, about 12 – 15 minutes.

While baking, watch carefully as they over-bake easily.

Makes about three dozen.

Delicious!

42 MAIN ST.
SHERBROOKE, NS

CHAPTER 8

SHERBROOKE, NOVA SCOTIA

SHERBROOKE VILLAGE

Gold and Lumber created this timeless Village

SHERBROOKE VILLAGE in Nova Scotia in 1860 was buzzing with activity. Today it looks almost exactly the same.

In 1861, gold was discovered in the area, and overnight, nineteen mining camps were built. Already busy were the lumbering mills buzzing to lathe products for England and the British West Indies.

The French were the first European settlers to arrive in the early 1600s and the area has been found to be a good location to settle ever since. By the 1860s the town was prosperous. There were churches, a school and eventually a busy Temperance society. Drunkenness was not tolerated.

Women donned elegant hooped dresses and shopped for fabrics and hats at the Cumminger Brothers General Store while men strolled the streets in their finest suits made by the local tailors for special occasions. There were lots of working types, trades and craftsmen around town, and a jail was opened for the unruly in a large home that served that purpose until 1969.

Sherbrooke is a unique place to visit as the buildings stand as they always have, remaining in the old section of the town. They have been restored to their era of glory. Visitors

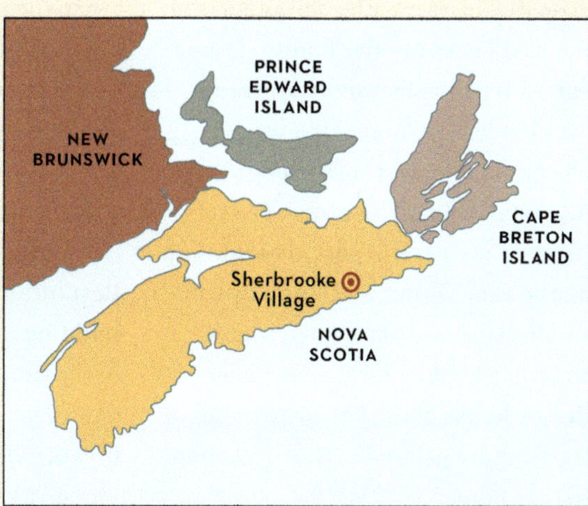

drop in and chat with characters from the past in twenty-five buildings and can watch the blacksmith working over the hot fire to repair a wagon wheel; see a weaver turn sheep's wool into fabric; observe a piece of wood turned into a useful part for a tall ship on the 1860s lathe; and stand by while small letters are placed in a frame to print a book or local newspaper. Recipe books of the favourite tastes of the time are printed in the print shop to take home.

In the jailhouse, cinnamon buns are baking in the woodstove and butter is made in a churn. Sit beside the jailhouse wife for a while and she will teach you how to bake like the women of the past.

McDaniel's Tea Room and Restaurant serves traditional fare in a building that used to serve the patrons of the time. Food such as corn and fish chowders, baked beans with brown bread, gingerbread and homemade pies give time travelers a taste of the

past. "Step Into 1867" gives visitors the chance to choose a period outfit from an extensive costume collection.

Strolling around old Sherbrooke village in a long hooped skirt and elegant bonnet or suit makes the visitor part of the village. And a cup of tea and piece of pie remind us of the timelessness of our tastes.

9

NO CINNAMON BUNS FOR DRUNKS

(Circa 1860s)

THE FRONT DOOR of the Sherbrooke jailhouse banged open causing Martha to fumble the pan of cinnamon buns she was putting in the woodstove.

Two unruly men and one unkempt woman stumbled through the door along with Martha's husband.

"Don't look like no jailhouse to me. Looks like a rich man's house," said one of them.

"Smells like heaven," said the other.

Only bars on the windows distinguished it from any other house in town.

Henry, the jailkeeper, told his wife to add more water to the soup pot.

"Don't feed em too well or they'll be back next week," grumbled Henry.

"I've heard of the food in this place," said Mabel Jones in a slurred voice.

The smell of cinnamon buns soon filled the house and Martha decided that such a treat would be a mite too tasty for the mischievous citizens keeping them company that night.

"Think I'll make a quick batch of biscuits," Martha said aloud.

Martha brought prisoner Mabel to help her in the kitchen.

"That's a mighty big, fancy stove you got there," said Mabel.

"Why that's my New Waterloo stove, came all the way from Lunenburg," said Martha with a look of pride. "Henry bought it with the pittance they pay him for work in the jail. He's at the sawmill now earnin more.

"Now, stop waggin your tongue and take this big mixing bowl, Mabel, and put in two teacups full of flour from that bin," ordered Martha, handing her the lard.

She gave her two knives and told her to cut the flour and lard together until they were like little white peas in the bowl.

"Now add these," she said as she put a bit of salt, and soda in Mabel's hands.

"And here's the secret: add this teacup of milk in a hole in the middle," and she dug with her finger and poured. "Take your wooden spoon, and mix it all together in just five strokes around the edge of the bowl. Not too much or we'll be serving rocks with the soup."

Martha showed Mabel how to knead the dough gently just enough to hold it together, shape it to a flattened round and roll it out to be two inches thick. Together they cut shapes with the open end of glasses and put them on the cooking sheet.

Out of the oven came the cinnamon rolls and in went the biscuits. Shouts came from the main floor cells.

"That cinnamon smells mighty good, ladies," whined two rowdy boys from their cells. "Can we try one?"

"Maybe when you've learned your lesson," said Martha, with a laugh.

Jail House Biscuits

4 Cups flour — *¾ C. shortening*

¾ Cup white sugar — *1 tsp. salt*

7 tsp. baking powder

2 eggs & enough milk to make 1¾ Cups

Mix first 5 ingredients together.
Put eggs & milk in a separate bowl.
Mix well. Add milk & eggs to mixture
and blend. Roll and cut.
Bake in 425 - 450 oven., 15 min.

Above is a recipe hand-printed at the village and included in the recipe book from Sherbrooke Village.

SHERBROOKE VILLAGE

CINNAMON BUNS

This recipe was told to me by a woman in 1800s costume, as she was baking. She would have known the recipe by memory.

- 4 cups flour
- ⅔ cup shortening
- dash salt
- 2 eggs
- 1 cup buttermilk
- butter
- brown sugar
- cinnamon

BEAT ALL INGREDIENTS together until they are of smooth consistency.

Pat the dough into a square shape and use a rolling pin to smooth the top.

Spread butter over the entire surface and sprinkle brown sugar over the surface, topping it all with cinnamon.

Roll the square with the open seam down.

Cut into slices and put in baking pan.

Bake at 350°F until done.

4568 HIGHWAY 12
CHESTER, NS

CHAPTER 9

NEW ROSS, NOVA SCOTIA

ROSS FARM MUSEUM

Still working the land

AT FIRST GLANCE, driving down the lane, the Ross Farm looks like many others in the countryside of Nova Scotia. Closer inspection reveals a team of oxen ploughing the fields, horses pulling a wagon, and women in long dresses and bonnets hanging laundry outside a wooden shingled home.

Members of the Ross family farmed this land for over one hundred and fifty years. In 1969, it was given to the Province of Nova Scotia by a family member and opened as a museum in 1970. Now, the Ross Farm is a year-round living history site that presents a real life farm experience in New Ross in the late 1800s. The farm proudly preserves the customs of the past to share with curious visitors and to keep the history of the area alive.

In 1816, Captain William Ross, his wife and a group of 172 soldiers settled in New Ross. Members of the disbanded Nova Scotia Fencible Infantry, the men were immigrants from Ireland, England, Scotland, Germany, and Italy. For their service, they were granted plots of land by the government to settle the interior of Nova Scotia. In order to keep the land, they had three years to clear it and render it productive.

Captain Ross and Mary Williams were married in Ireland and had five

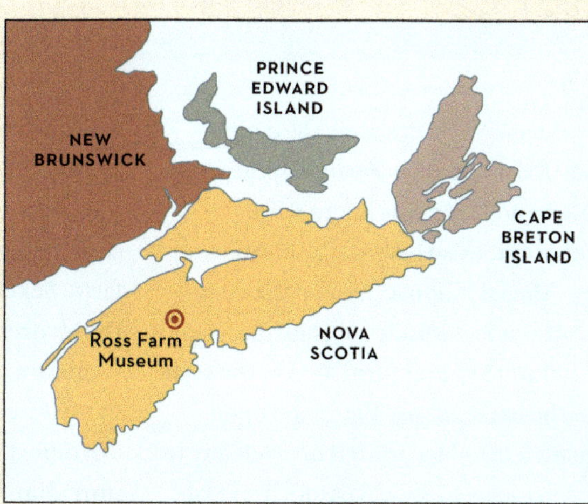

children. Six years after the couple settled at the Ross Farm, Captain Ross died and Mary was left to work the farm and raise her family on her own.

The farmhouse, named Rosebank Cottage, is a wooden shingled cottage built in 1817 and furnished in the style of the early 1800s. The grand open-hearth fireplace is fired up each day to cook meals to show visitors how it was done in a time when the family worked hard to put food on the table. Authentically cooked meals include seasonal and preserved food from the farm. Baked beans, biscuits, pies made in Dutch ovens, sauerkraut, sausages and soups are among the foods still cooked in the kitchen. Food preservation was an important cooking skill crucial for providing food through the winter.

The farm continues to work the land with teams of oxen and horses, and raises heritage breeds of sheep, cattle and chickens. A working stave mill and cooperage demonstrate the barrel-making industry that flourished in this area. Gardens are planted with heritage vegetables, and the orchard grows several varieties of apples.

At the end of each day, members of the Ross family and their workers sat down together in the kitchen to enjoy the food they raised and grew, as the farm gates closed on another day's hard work.

THE WORK GOES ON . . .

Ross Farm, Autumn 1827

CABBAGE BITS FLEW all over the kitchen at Rosebank Cottage and the sound of knives chopping cabbage was like a marching band. Mary's kitchen was full of friends from the neighbouring farms and it was sauer-kraut-making time. She looked at the women working furiously in front of the open hearth fireplace, and thought it was a wonder they didn't chop their hands off, so fierce was the chatting and gossiping. After chopping the cabbage they would pound in the salt and put the mixture in barrels, weighing it all down with rocks. Time did the rest of the work.

"Remind me why this is the day we must make the sauerkraut?" Little Mary asked her mother.

"Because my grandmother taught me and her grandmother taught her and her grandmother taught her, that sauerkraut has to be made only when the moon is growing. You count five days after the new moon and that is when you make the sauerkraut, and that is all there is to it."

The cabbage crop was good that year and they had lots of work ahead of them putting it down, because after all, what was a meal without sauerkraut?

Mary told Little Mary how her grandmother had preached the health benefits of sauerkraut.

"It saved our sailors from the horrible scurvy." Plugging her nose, Little Mary ate the sour stringy dish.

Mary took a moment to rest and looked out the window across the farm. The rest of the farm was buzzing with activity. Today, the men were working in the cooperage making barrels, for it was harvest time. It had been two years since her husband William had gone to the angels, and she was grateful that she had four fine sons and so many friends to help her continue to run the farm. There were the crops to plant and harvest, the animals to care for, and barrels to make. Life ahead was going to be more work than she could ever have imagined.

She remembered the nights of sitting down to dinner in front of a blazing fire after the hard days of work it took to clear the land. They would enjoy beef stew, sauerkraut, some homemade bread and an Apple Pan Dowdy for dessert. That was when William was alive, and life was perfect.

Now, Mary focused back on the life in front of her and decided to make William's favourite dessert for her workers' dinner. She trudged out through the fields to pick windfall apples from the ground and piled them in her apron. Back in the kitchen she peeled the apples, made the sauce and poured it over the apples in the pie pan, covering it with a doughy mixture. That was the way her mama made it and she would be sure to teach Little Mary that favourite as well.

Mary laid the table with extra care that night adding a candle and flowers from the field. The men could smell the Dowdy cooking all the way out to the cooperage and they all rushed in the door at once at dinnertime.

Each man took his place at the table and the children squeezed in between.

"Are we expecting a guest? Little Mary asked, noticing the empty seat at the head of the table.

"Tonight we set a place for your father," Mary said, wiping away a tear. "This being his favourite dinner, and he loved to see us all around the table after a hard day. Many hands make light work, your father always said."

At that moment the candle in the middle of the table flickered and Mary's heart warmed as she looked across the table full of food, family and friends. She winked at William's empty chair at the end of the table.

SAUERKRAUT

Recipe courtesy of Ross Farm

- 10-12 good sized cabbages (winter cabbages)
- 1½ pints salt

ALWAYS PREPARED WHEN the moon was growing, the cabbage would be shredded using a kraut knife and placed in a barrel, alternately with layers of salt. A half barrel filled ⅔ full of shredded cabbage would require 1½ pints of salt.

The cabbage would be stomped with a wooden stomper as each layer added. When finished, a weight is placed on the kraut to keep it under the brine once it starts to work. After about three weeks, the kraut would be ready to eat or stored in the cellar for winter use.

Sauerkraut complements pork chops, ham and sausage and can also be fried with pork chops.

APPLE PAN DOWDY

Recipe courtesy of Ross Farm

SAUCE

- 1 cup brown sugar
- ¼ cup flour
- 1 Tbsp vinegar
- 1½ cups water
- 1 Tbsp butter
- 1 tsp vanilla

BATTER

- 3 Tbsp shortening
- ½ tsp salt
- 1 cup flour
- ½ cup milk
- 2 tsp baking powder

SLICE 4 OR 5 APPLES in bottom of well-greased casserole dish, pour sauce over apples.

Add nutmeg & cinnamon to apples. In a bowl, cream shortening like pastry with flour, salt and baking powder.

Mix in milk.

Drop on top of apple & sauce mixture.

Bake at 350°F for about ½ hour.

Good with whipped cream, ice cream or as is.

5795 AFRICVILLE RD.
HALIFAX, NS

CHAPTER 10

HALIFAX, NOVA SCOTIA

AFRICVILLE MUSEUM

A Vibrant Community Lives On

ON THE FAR side of the tracks, beside the huge freighters docked in the Bedford Basin, there is a park. Amidst the trees sits a small church; that is what is left of Africville.

The Africville National Historic Site is an oasis of calm and dignity in the industrial, harbour area of Halifax, Nova Scotia. It was once a colourful, vibrant and closely woven community of small brightly painted homes, clustered on a hill sloping down to the water.

During a history dating back to 1745, Africville was home to families who were descendants of Black Loyalists, Jamaican Maroons, and Black Refugees.

In Africville, families established homes, businesses and farms, and residents were known to take great pride in their homes. A former resident, Leon Steed said, "To us it was heaven, a real home."

The Seaview Baptist Church was the foundation of the community, both spiritually and socially, and families attended services regularly. The custom was to enjoy Sunday dinner after church with family and friends.

Each household paid taxes to the city of Halifax, but residents of Africville had no clean drinking water, sewers, or garbage collection—though

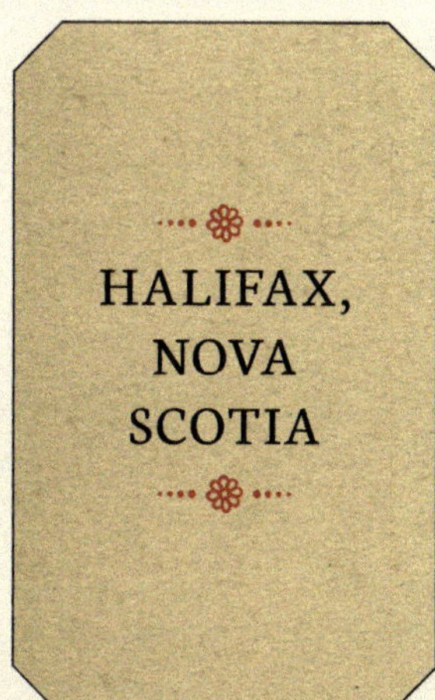

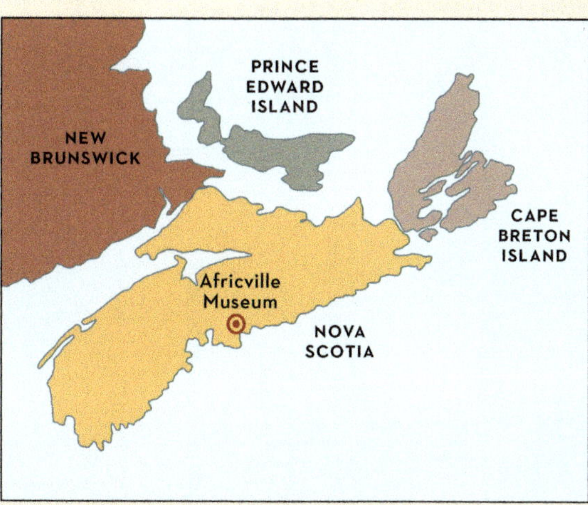

all of these were offered to the residents of Halifax at that time. The area housed a prison, a dump, and an infectious disease hospital for the city, and was labeled "a slum".

The residents of Africville protested their lack of services for many years but despite all their efforts to maintain and improve their community, their homes were bulldozed and the settlement was destroyed between 1964 and 1969, to make room for industrial expansion. People were forced to relocate to different parts of the city, and in the end their sense of community was lost.

In 2010, the city of Halifax finally made a public apology along with a financial settlement, and donated a two-and-a-half-acre plot of land as compensation. The community used the money and land to reconstruct the Seaview Baptist Church, which now serves as a museum telling the history of Africville. A guided tour, large storyboards and relics from the past, tell the compelling story of families, homes and community lost.

A cookbook, *In the Africville Kitchens, The Comforts of Home*, was compiled in 2020, and it tells the story of Africville while featuring favourite recipes. This project was undertaken to pull people together and has been hugely successful, for this is a community that still enjoys sharing meals together.

Although the descendants of those who originated from Africa and the Caribbean have blended their tastes with changing times, recipes and the spirit of sharing food continue to be handed down through the generations. The pulse of the Africville heart can still be felt in that little church surrounded by the bustle of industry in Halifax; it was and is still strong.

Entrance
To
SEAVIEW PARK
City of Halifax

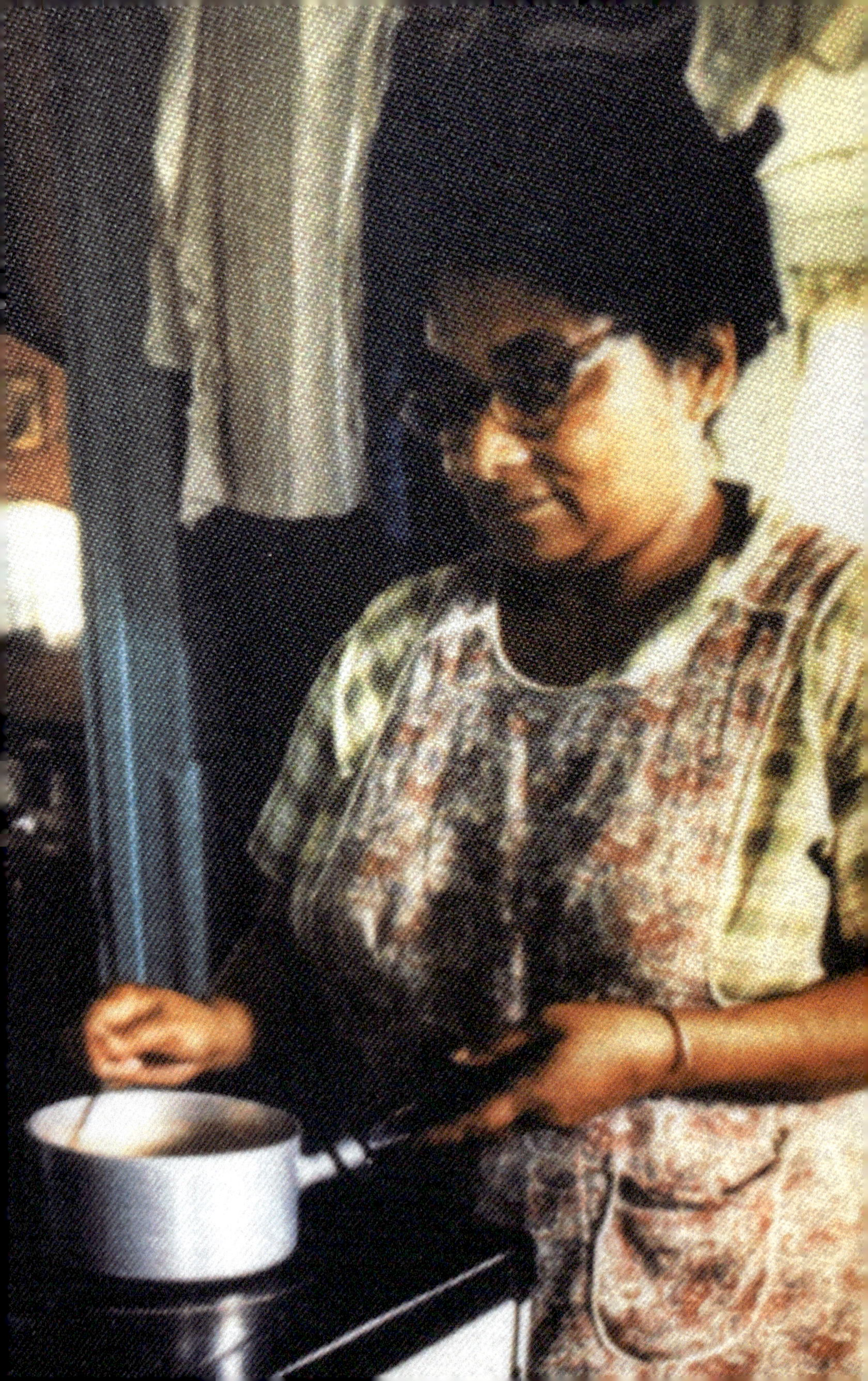

MAKING THE BEST OF EVERYTHING

Africville, Nova Scotia 1965

IT WAS THE blue flowered china that changed Mum. She had always loved cooking but once we were made to move from our little yellow clapboard cabin in Africville to the blue house on the other side of town, things changed. We loved our little yellow home and did not want to move, but we had no choice. Our neighbours were gone, our town was gone, and everything we knew was gone.

"We're just gonna move," said Mum because she always made the best of everything.

Mum walked into the kitchen of our new blue house, opened the cupboards and found a whole set of dishes, just sitting there. Not just any dishes, but dishes that all matched, and lots of them, with no chips or cracks or worn spots , and blue like the house, with flowers. The old woman that lived there died and just up and left all the china. Just a stroke of luck. Who knew that dishes could make Mum that happy? In our yellow home in Africville we ate our food from chipped dishes, all different, and I liked them. I could pick my favourite one everyday and we kids would fight over the ones with the most colour.

"Come and help me, little one," Mum would say to me. " What I will teach you are the cooking ways of our folks, your grandma, her Mum, her Grandma and like that forever. You've gotta share these tastes with your children and they with their children. This is not written in words; these tastes are in the soul and they come all the way from Africa."

I asked her where Africa was, and she just shook her head and kept on singing.

One Saturday she was in the kitchen making our Sunday dinner. Fish cakes again, but I wouldn't dare complain. I saw her cutting the potatoes, the turnip and the onions, and soaking the cod.

My Mum looked at me with love and said, "Boy, we've gotta use what we got. And we're gonna invite our neigbour over. "

"But we don't like that man," I remember tellin my Mum.

"You know, son," she said gently, "old Benny Slimms used to say, 'If you are mad at your neighbour or friend, invite him in and sit him down and give him something to eat and pray for him.' And that's just what we're

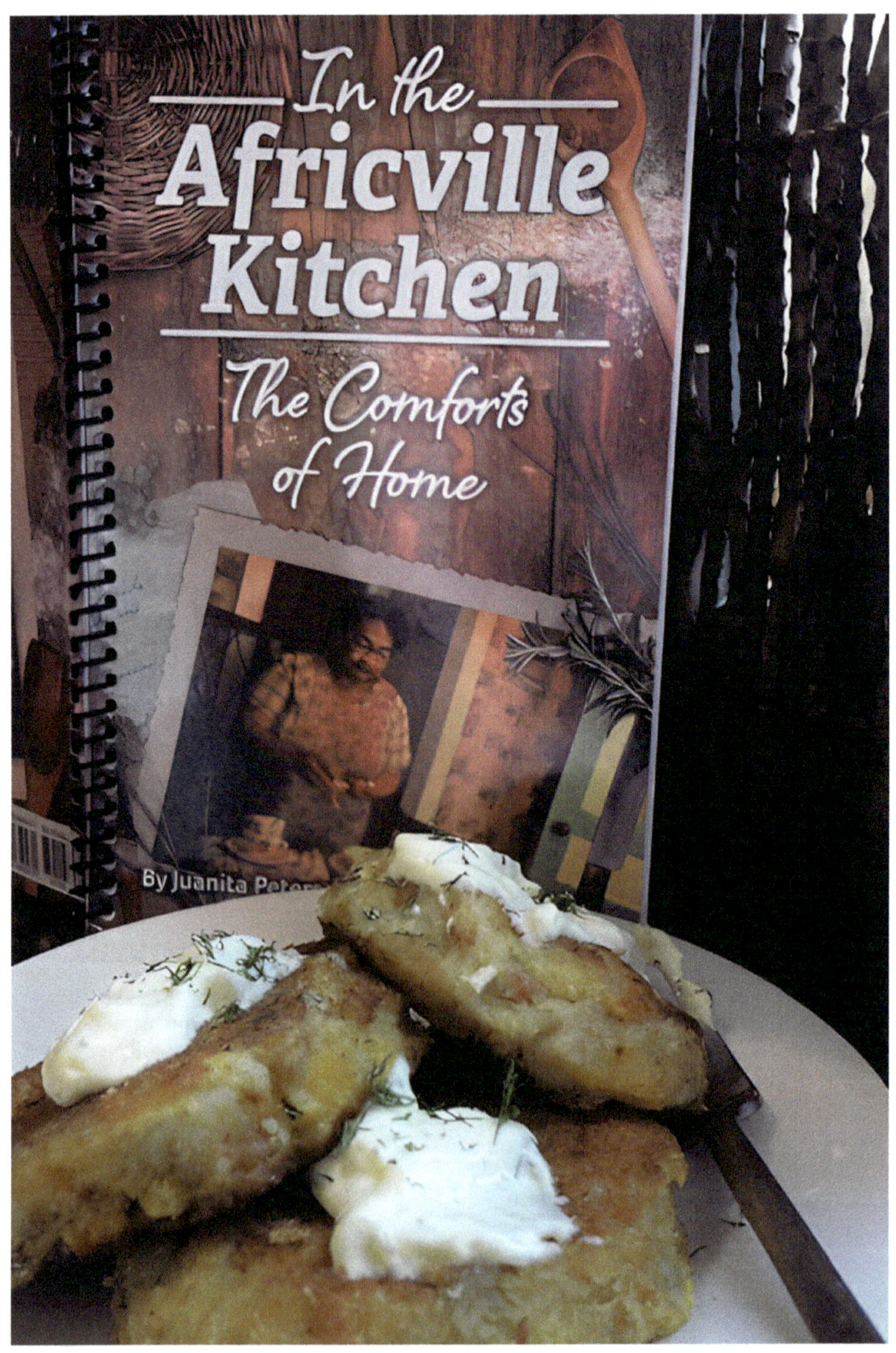

Photos courtesy of Africville Museum.

going to do," she said firmly as she set the table with the new dishes. "And there'll be blueberry grunt for the ones that clean their blue plates."

Mum could take whatever food God gave her any day and turn it into a feast.But that Sunday when she got out those shiny blue flowered plates and piled on the fish cakes, all those around our family table fell silent. And the neighbour that we didn't like, smiled big.

"Thank you God for all we got," my Mum said, and we all answered, "Amen."

BLUEBERRY GRUNT

Both recipes with permission from
In the Africville Kitchen, the Comforts of Home
As submitted by Olive Cassidy.

- 2 cups blueberries
- 1¾ tsp baking powder
- 1½ cups water
- 1 Tbsp shortening
- ⅔ cup sugar
- ⅓ cup milk or more
- 4 tsp salt
- 2 cups flour

PREHEAT THE OVEN to 400°F.

Pick over and wash the blueberries. Put them in a greased pan. Add in water and sugar and put in the oven for 5 minutes.

While it's cooking, mix the salt, baking powder, and flour in a big bowl. Cut the shortening into the flour mixture with a knife.

Add milk to make a soft dough, handling the dough as little as possible and mix. Drop in spoonfuls of the dough into the baked blueberry mixture.

Cover and cook for about 25 minutes.

NEE'S FISH CAKES

Submitted by Paula Grant-Smith in memory of her mother Rose Lenoir-Grant

- 3-4 large potatoes
- 2 Tbsp of parsley
- 1 medium turnip
- Bread crumbs
- 3-4 bags of salt cod fish
- 2 eggs
- Butter
- Pepper and Garlic
- 2 onions
- Vegetable oil for frying

PUT SALT COD in cold water to soak. Drain water continuously until you determine how salty you want it before boiling.

She would boil the fish and check for saltiness as well, continuously changing the water until satisfied. When fish and potatoes and turnip are cooked, mash. Flake fish.

Add all ingredients together and mould into patties. Heat oil in a large skillet over a medium high heat. Fry the patties on both sides until golden brown. Drain on paper towel before serving. Enjoy!

121 BLUENOSE DR.
LUNENBURG, NS

CHAPTER 11

LUNENBURG, NOVA SCOTIA (OR WHEREVER SHE IS SAILING)

BLUENOSE II

"And never had such a spectacle graced the Nova Scotia Coast" - Beaton

WHEN SHE IS not sailing the seas, the schooner Bluenose II rests in the water beside a dock in Lunenburg, in all her glory. The beauty and grace of this schooner's lines are stunning. When she is dockside visitors are invited aboard to see what life was like on this fishing and racing vessel. On the deck rests a copy of a Typical Saltbanker Menu by Captain Angus Tanner. This copy of a handwritten menu recalls the days when the original Bluenose was a fishing vessel, and allows visitors to imagine sharing the table below with the fishermen. Dishes such as Kartoffelsuppe, Scouse, Hurricane Soup, Fish Eyes, House Banking and Hagdown Pot Pie made for an exotic menu with a nod to the German influence of the area.

The original Bluenose was built in 1921 in Lunenburg, Nova Scotia. Racing was important to her owners, and one season of fishing the Grand Banks was a requirement before participating in The International series of races. When the races were held, Bluenose won every year for seventeen years. Bluenose was used to fish and race until the 1930s. Captain Angus J. Walters was the first to sail Bluenose with 21 crew, including 16 dorymen, 4 dressing (salting) crew, and a cook.

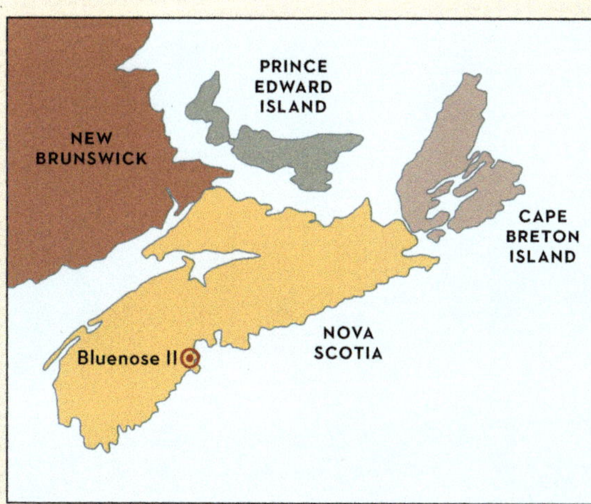

Preparing meals for the hard-working fishermen was a demanding job as the cook made four huge meals a day in the tiny kitchen below a deck that never stood still.

The men lived on the ship from April to September, making as many as six trips during a season to fish the Banks off the coast of Newfoundland and Nova Scotia. The men would take dories out before daylight and lay lines of ropes connected to a buoy to which were attached hooks that hung below. The dories went out several more times during the day to pull in the fish, and return the catch to the ship where the dressing crew cleaned and threw the fish below to be salted.

By the time the Depression hit in the 1930's, Bluenose had become a national symbol, was motorized and had become a touring vessel. Over time, fishing schooners were replaced by engine-powered ships, and in 1942, the schooner was sold to the West Indies Trading Company. The sails were removed and she was used to carry freight until 1946, when she ran aground on a coral reef near Haiti.

Bluenose II is a replica of the original, built in 1963 by many of the original ship builders. She has functioned since then as a sailing ambassador. In 2009 an extensive overhaul was done to repair the boat and she was relaunched in 2015. The kitchen below has changed since the days of the original Bluenose and now the table where the fishermen once dined has been recreated using wood from each province of Canada.

JOHN BEATON WROTE IN HIS POEM,
TO THE BLUENOSE:

And never had such a spectacle graced
the Nova Scotian coast
as your flying jib off Lunenburg.

BLUENOSE

Robert Herman, cook on Bluenose 1936, photo courtesy of the Nova Scotia Museum.

BETTER FISH THAN COOK

Grand Banks - Atlantic Ocean, 1924.

IT WAS a foggy day and the waters were rough. Very rough.

It was Eddie's first day as part of the crew on Bluenose. He was young, and from a farming family, but Captain would give him a chance as a flunky to run errands wherever he was needed. He watched the other fellas head out in their dories at four this morning to put out the lines with hooks. Eddie was sent down below to help the salters but he could hardly hold down last night's Mug Up so the salters sent him to help in the kitchen.

Eddie was "quite green" when he climbed into the mess cabin, noted the cook, who could barely take the time to look at him.

"Not feeling too great," said Eddie.

Cook knew it was Eddie's first trip so he tried to show a bit of kindness.

"Well, stick with me and you can help cook for the other boys, whadda you think? Best friend to make on this ship is me," said the cook.

Eddie could smell food cooking for the day. He admired how Cook juggled the pots, pans, and all the ingredients that would go into today's chow, all while the boat tossed from side to side.

For breakfast, the boys would have beans that were baked on the stove. The cook was frying leftover potatoes into hash, and scouse was bubbling away on the stove.

"What's scouse?" asked Eddie.

"Like a stew," said Cook, made from all the meats and vegetables left over from other meals. As if that weren't enough, Cook was making biscuits to be baked and slicing up a loaf of bread he had made the day before.

Just the thought of the food made Eddie's stomach turn.

Cook put Eddie right to work.

"You can roll the pie crust for the pumpkin pie for dinner at noon. And peel them potatoes, we need 'em for every meal. We need 'em for the hash and the fish chowder for supper and the Kartoffelsuppe for tomorrow.

"Does you know how to knead bread, boy?" the cook asked hopefully.

Eddie worked so hard that day that he didn't have time to think about the rough seas—indeed, he figured he had never worked so hard in his life as the day he helped Cook.

"Them boys eat all day," he said to Cook.

"The more they eats, the harder they work, the more fish we gets," said Cook.

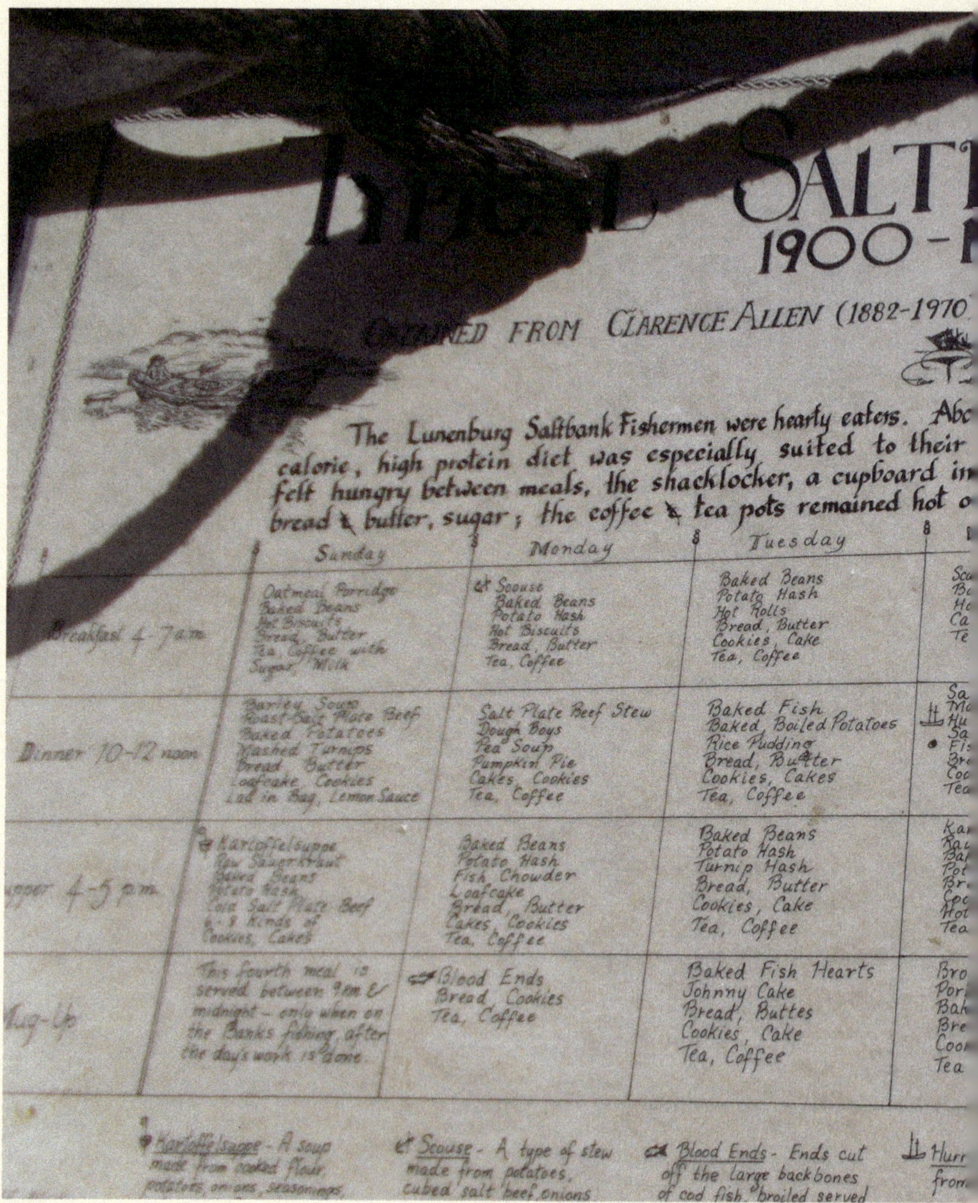

Mug Up was the last eats of the day and before bed and the men could have all the bread, cookies, tea and coffee they wanted. After Eddie helped Cook serve and clean up the last of the Mug Up, he fell fast asleep in his bunk.

But he was the first man up the next morning, and he planned to brave out the seas while helping the salters today. "Cook be on his own today" he

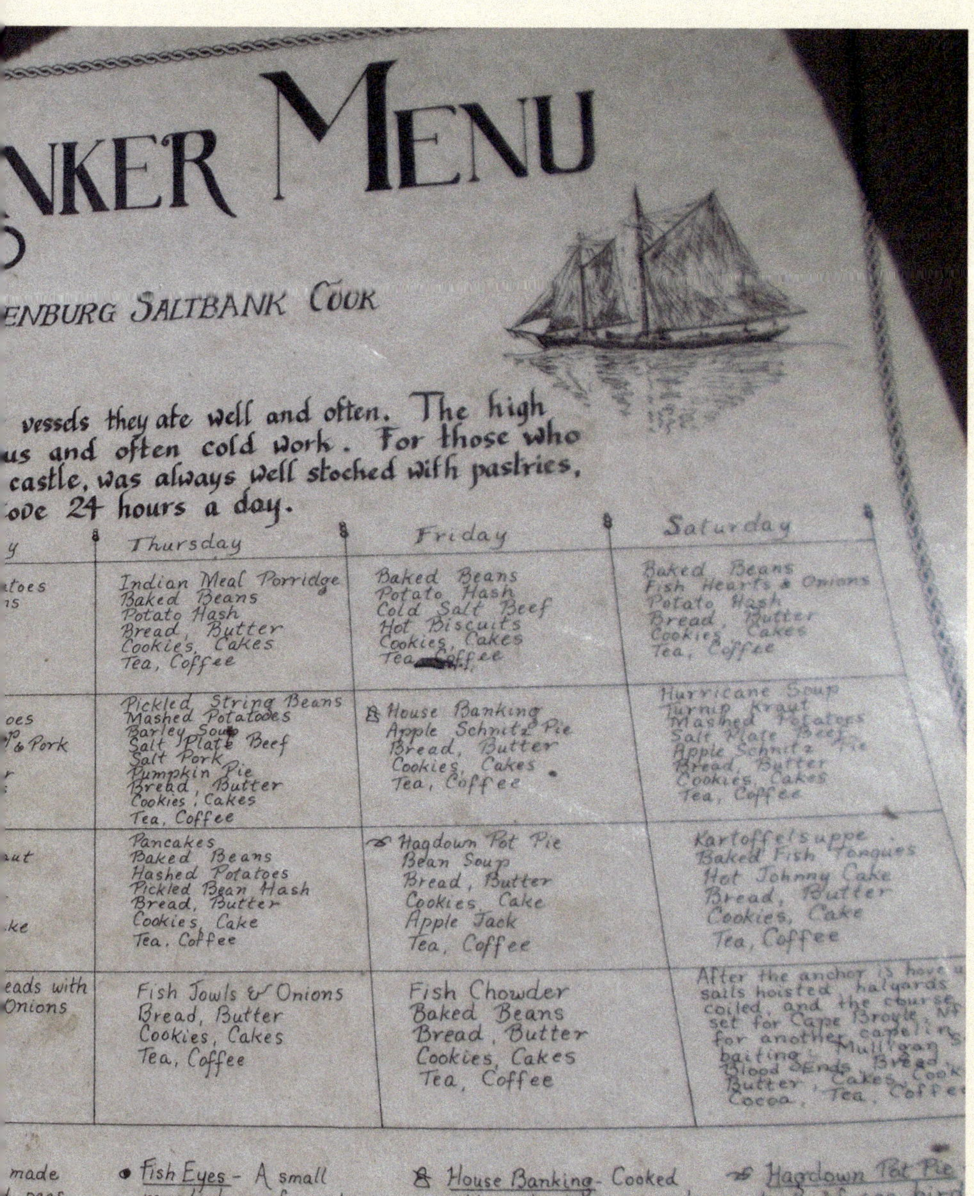

thought as he headed down below where the salting was done. Didn't even let Cook see him leave.

He could hardly wait for his breakfast.

KARTOFFELSUPPE

FROM DUTCH OVEN

A CookBook of coveted, traditional Recipes from the Kitchens of Lunenburg.
Contributed by Ada S. Stebb.

- 1 quart diced potatoes
- 1 tsp pepper
- 2 quarts water
- 3 oz sheer fat pork
- 1 large onion
- 6 Tbsp flour
- 2 tsp salt

CUT PORK IN small cubes and fry until light brown.

When slightly cool put in pot with potatoes, water and onion and cook until potatoes are soft.

Put flour in pan where pork was fried and brown it, stirring constantly.

Add the browned flour to soup and stir until the flour is dissolved.

Add seasonings and boil one minute.

Serve a small dish of sauerkraut with each serving of soup.

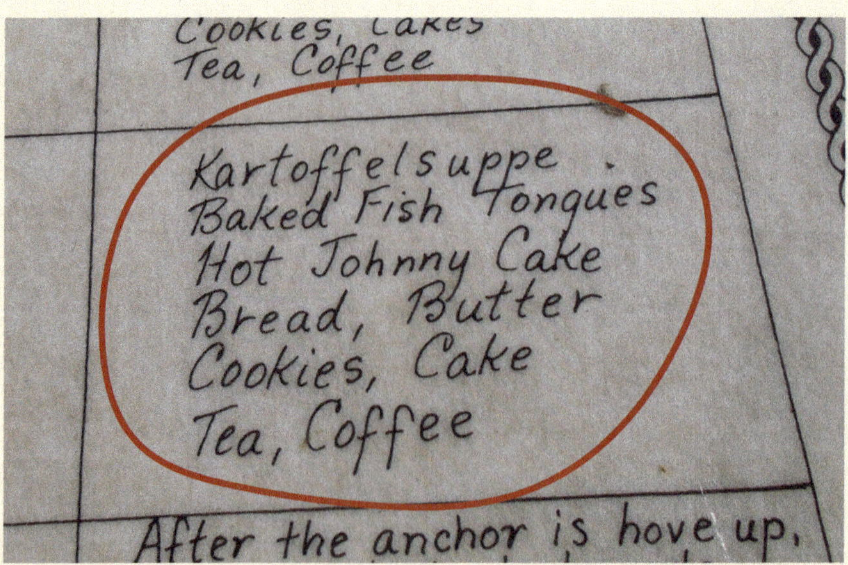

HOSKING STORE
POST OFFICE
OPEN

5435 CLAM HARBOUR RD.
LAKE CHARLOTTE, NS

CHAPTER 12

LAKE CHARLOTTE, NOVA SCOTIA

MEMORY LANE HERITAGE VILLAGE

A community moving into the 1940's

The old Hooking General Store is a wandering drive down the east coast of Nova Scotia to Lake Charlotte. Inside, the shelves are piled high with intriguing goods from the past. Visitors walking through the back door of the shop emerge into the community of Lake Charlotte, circa 1940. The gears of time shift smoothly when a 1928 Ford Model A stops to offer a ride around Memory Lane; it's a slow drive, and a fitting reminder that life did not move as quickly back then.

Memory Lane Heritage Village is a community project created in the year 2000 to save important heritage buildings along the Eastern shore that were slated to be torn down. The structures were relocated to the site that has become Memory Lane, a small village that conjures up a different time.

This living history museum is the pride of the Lake Charlotte community. Here, the work of over 200 volunteers preserves and celebrates life in the 1940s. Pump organ music plays quietly in the church. The Prospector's cabin looks as though the inhabitant just stepped out for a moment. In the Fisherman's Storehouse, nets are being made and interesting old fishing tools clutter the walls.

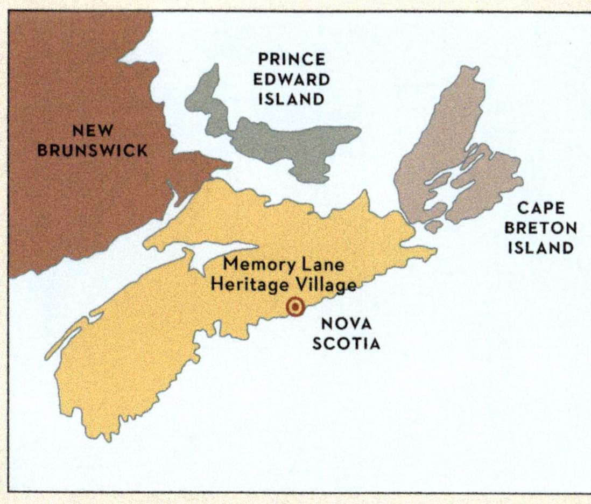

Before electricity arrived in Lake Charlotte in 1945, ice was brought in big pieces from nearby lakes and rivers, and stored in sawdust in the community ice house. Families came with tongs to bring home large chunks for their iceboxes.

The Webber House shows how a home was transformed after electricity arrived. Furnished as it would have been in the forties, the home feels as though the family has left the doors unlocked and gone for a drive, but will be back soon. Red long johns dance on the clothesline, drying quickly in the sun and wind.

The irresistible smell of fresh bread wafts from the Cookhouse. There were many mining and lumber camps in this area in the early 1900s, and the workers were well fed. Memory Lane offers the chance to eat like a logger and taste timeless East Coast meals. The lumber camp cookhouse serves up a hot meal and cold salad plate, both fit for a lumberjack. Visitors dine on benches at long tables as the hungry lumbermen or miners would have done. The rules posted on the cookhouse walls advise guests to scrape their plates and deliver them to be washed. Visitors leave with bellies full of great food, and the lingering taste of nostalgia.

Take your time, slow down is the message Memory Lane whispers to departing guests.

ICE CREAM MEMORIES

It was a hot, lazy summer day in 1942 in Oyster Pond, Nova Scotia.

" Follow me, Mr. Webber," shouted young Jimmy who had just burst through the door. "Mom's making ice cream and she said to come and watch."

"Ice cream, well I'll be darned," said Irvine.

Irvine was a shy and quiet man who lived on his own and he didn't usually go a callin. But he did love ice cream more than anything, and so he followed the boy to his house down the road.

Irvine found Gertie Mitchell sweating and out of breath as she turned the crank on a wooden bucket. "Here, take over," she said, "just keep turning it. William picked up this ice cream maker when he was sellin' wood down the coast."

Irvine wanted to know every detail about how this mysterious wooden bucket with the crank on the top worked.

"Lots of work," said Gertie. " First you get some good thick cream, a few eggs, some sugar and make a custard on the stovetop. You pour the custard into the metal container and set it inside the bucket. Then you have to run over and get a hunk of ice from the icehouse, hammer it until it breaks into small pieces and pack it around inside the container with some rock salt. Put on the top and start cranking, and cranking. When the crank gets hard to turn, you know you've got ice cream. Open it up and eat. Fast. Before it melts in this godforsaken heat."

Irvine couldn't believe you could make ice cream in the middle of summer.

Gertie Mitchell was known around Oyster Pond as a good cook. He knew Gertie because she cooked for the men out at the lumber camp in the winter. Irvine always wished for a wife, but it never happened, so food was pretty simple at his house. He looked forward to winter at the lumber camp, where he could have mighty good meals. He loved the smell of fresh bread when he walked in the door of the cookhouse. They ate well: baked beans, fresh bread, sausages, fruit pies, and it made the hard work worth it. He would sit on the long bench with his buddies and eat and eat. There were rules though; they had to scrape their plates and deliver them to the kitchen when they were done. You wouldn't dare break a rule – the food was too good.

But now it was the middle of a very hot summer, and Irvine wiped the sweat from his brow. Cranking ice cream was some hard work but all was forgotten when the bowl topped with fresh strawberries was put in front of him. On his way out the door, Gertie handed him a bowl of leftover beans and a few pieces of bread and told him to take it home for his dinner.

"That ice cream was some good," said Irvine, and gave Gertie a peck on the cheek.

When Irvine walked past Hosking's General Store on his way home he remembered the day his Pappy took him to the ice cream parlour above the store when he was a boy. It was long gone now but back then, Roxie the owner had the best ice cream in the world. She told him it came all the way by train and wagon from Halifax to her parlour which made it taste even better.

"Maybe I should get myself one of them ice cream makers," he whispered to himself.

Oyster Pond, he thought, might just be the best place in the world to live.

VANILLA ICE CREAM

From Out of Old Nova Scotia Kitchens by Marie Nightingale.

- 2 quarts milk
- 2 Tbsp flour
- 4 eggs, well beaten
- 4 cups sweet cream (cold)
- 2 cups sugar
- 1 tsp vanilla

SCALD THE MILK over hot water. Add well beaten eggs, sugar and flour.

Mix well and let cook for about 30 minutes, stirring occasionally.

Remove from heat and chill thoroughly. Beat the mixture well with a rotary beater and add the cream and vanilla.

Pour into prepared freezer and turn it for 15 to 20 minutes until the turning process becomes difficult. Remove dasher and pack the ice cream down firmly.

Then re-pack the freezer with ice and freezing salt, allowing 1 part salt to 8 parts ice.

Cover the freezer with an old blanket and layers of newspaper and allow to set for an hour or two. This will further harden the ice cream and ripen it.

BAKED BEANS

As they might have eaten in the lumber camp.

- 1 pound dried beans
- 1 tsp salt
- ½ Tbsp mustard
- ⅛ tsp pepper
- ⅓ cup brown sugar
- 1 pound diced salt pork
- ¼ cup molasses
- 1 medium onion

SOAK THE BEANS overnight in plenty of water to cover.

The next day, parboil gently for 1½ hours. Drain and place in bean crock with mustard, sugar, molasses, salt, pepper and salt pork. Stir well and add just enough water to cover.

Place the onion on top and bake in a slow oven (300°F) for 6 to 8 hours, covered.

Add boiling water two or three times to keep beans moist. Uncover the last hour to brown, if desired. Do not add water during the last hour.

505 ROMA POINT RD.
THREE RIVERS, PE

CHAPTER 13

THREE RIVERS, PRINCE EDWARD ISLAND

JEAN-PIERRE ROMA NATIONAL HISTORIC SITE

A French Trading Colony in the New World

NEXT TO THE OCEAN, at the end of the red dirt Roma Point Road, is the Pierre Roma National Historic Site at Trois Rivières, Prince Edward Island. Here, visitors follow the scent of baking bread past a thriving garden towards buildings that conjure up another time.

In 1732, three boats arrived from France, carrying eighty travellers. On this site, Parisian Jean Pierre Roma established his colony as an international trading centre. Now visitors can taste a bit of their history at an eatery, visit replica buildings, and talk to costumed interpretive staff performing daily tasks as they would have done in the past. The Mi'kmaq would have played a role in the lives of the settlers and are an important part of the Roma settlement story.

The settlement has been reconstructed to 1732, based on the findings of archeological digs. Foundations and over seven thousand relics were unearthed that reveal much about everyday life in Pierre Roma's time. Clues such as a chocolate pouring vessel tell us that a beverage was made from chocolate traded from the West Indies. Originally there were buildings for housing, storehouses to contain

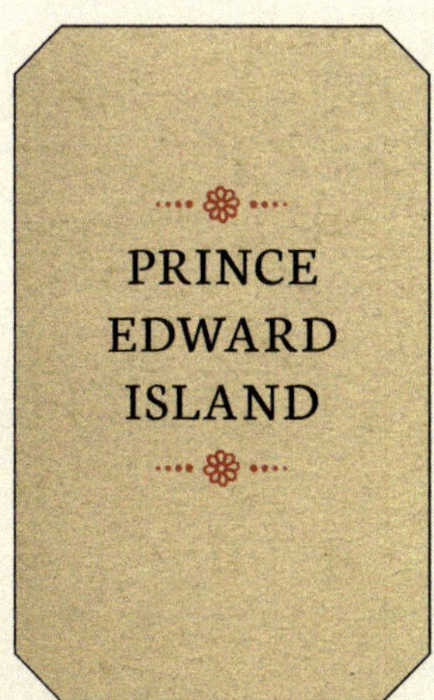

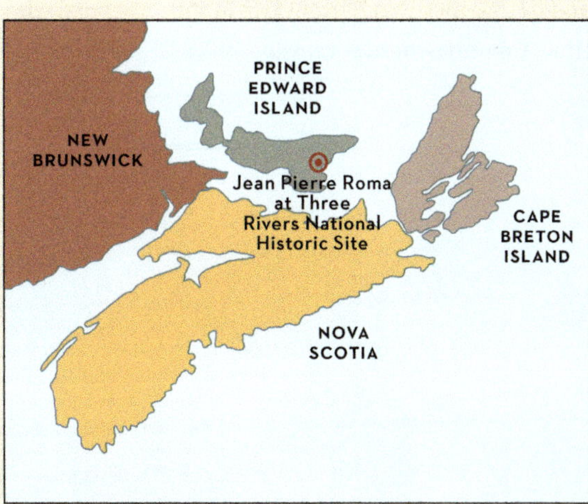

the trading goods, a bakery, a forge, large gardens and farm fields. An underground tunnel was discovered that led from the Roma house to the docks, and many old rum bottles were unearthed.

Pierre Roma was a clever trader who had lived and worked in the Caribbean earlier in his life and brought his skills to Trois Rivières. His trading route took salted cod to be used on the plantations of the West Indies, returning with sugar, molasses, rum and chocolate. He then traded and sold salted fish to France, bringing back Bordeaux wine. Goods were also traded with Fortress Louisbourg and Quebec.

After just thirteen years, the settlement was burned to the ground by British privateers. Jean Pierre and his children fled to nearby forests, eventually making their way to Quebec.

Now we can visit a large garden that recreates the culinary preferences and herbal medicinal practices of the time. Colonists here grew vegetables such as peas, turnips, radishes, beets, parsnips, Jerusalem artichokes, lettuce, cucumbers and chicory. They grew wheat and oats, among other grains, to be milled for bread making. Each worker was given three pounds of bread a day that was usually eaten with soup or fish chowder. Domesticated animals provided dairy and poultry products, and hunting and fishing for wild game and fish supplemented the meat.

Nowadays, bread is baked daily in the large replica red clay outdoor oven and sold to visitors. An eatery serves heritage meals and afternoon tea; dishes such as pea soup, creamy carrot and parsnip soup, fish cakes and pulled pork are served on long wooden tables. Fresh-baked bread accompanies the meals. Ginger cookies and chocolate cake are popular desserts.

A stroll through the buildings, and a taste of meals reminiscent of the past, bring to vivid life the legacy of those who left France for Roma's Trois Rivières settlement.

Photo of Chocolate making at Fortress Louisbourg.

A TASTE OF HOT CHOCOLATE TO CURE SEA LEGS

The year is 1735 on the Ile of St. Jean, (now Prince Edward Island)

JACQUES STUMBLED DOWN the gangplank after his long sea voyage from France to Trois Rivières. The waves had tossed him about for weeks and he could hardly walk on solid ground. The first thing he smelled was fresh bread baking. And that's why he had been sent here from prison- to assist the baker.

Young Marie Anne had watched the ship sail in, excited to see the newcomers. She dreamt of a playmate but knew that her father, Pierre Roma, had established this colony by bringing workers, and those arriving from France were here only to work.

Her eyes settled on a young man, guessing he might be fourteen.

"I am Marie Anne Roma, follow me," she said to Jacques, " you must be here to help the baker."

"How did you know?"

She just smiled and winked. "No playmate," she thought, "but he will just have to do."

As they trudged the hill from the docks, on their way to the oven, the smell of bread grew stronger. On the seas, Jacques had eaten nothing but dried ship's biscuits and soup for weeks.

"Bonjour," greeted the baker without looking away from his work, kneading the bread and forming round loaves. Marie Anne broke a piece from a warm loaf and handed it to Jacques. He had not tasted bread such as this since the day he had stolen a loaf from a Madame's basket back in France. Hardship had forced him to steal to bring home food for his brothers and sisters. That was also the day he was dragged off to jail. Later, some young prisoners were chosen to serve their punishment by working at Pierre Roma's settlement in New France. Now, for a moment he thought he had sailed to heaven. It was warm and dry, everything was green and he had been given a piece of tasty bread.

"You'll work plenty hard starting tomorrow," said the baker firmly, finally looking at Jacques. "We start before the sun rises, to mix and knead the dough to make beaucoup des pains. You will cut wood and tend the fire and work hard to pay for your sinful deeds. Now show him around ma petite cher," he instructed Marie Anne, "and then let him rest up."

Marie Anne started to run and motioned for Jacques to follow her. She showed him the garden and picked her favourite plants explaining carefully how each one was used to cure the ills of the men.

The storeroom was next, as she pointed to all the goods that had come from the trading ships and stuck her finger in a barrel of molasses for a lick of sweetness.

"Go ahead," she said. "Try it, you won't get in trouble."

The men were busy at the iron-works and didn't cast a glance their way. Some men were busy hanging fish and salting the cod. Others hid behind some barrels and were sneaking a drink of what smelled like rum. Marie Anne pointed to the fields and workers and said, "Too far to walk with your sea legs, but that's where the vegetables are grown and the wheat for your bread..."

Jacques stopped listening.

"I'm tired and hungry," Jacques finally pleaded as they headed for a large building.

"This is where my family lives and also it is a storehouse," said Marie Anne.

As they stepped in the door, Jacques knew for sure he was in heaven as the fire warmed his chilled hands and he smelled a sweet aroma unknown to him.

"Sit, you poor thing, "ordered a woman huddled over a pot by the fire. She was quickly rubbing a wooden tool vigorously between her hands. Then she poured a thick, brown mixture from an elegant chocolate server into two small cups, handing one to each of them.

"Chocolate," Marie Anne said as she noticed the puzzled look on his face.

"Shhhh. This, mon cher garçon, is a special drink for the master," advised the kind woman.

"I will spoil you just this once."

HOT CHOCOLATE BACK IN TIME

Recipe such as might have been served at Jean-Pierre Roma Historic Site

CHOCOLATE IS OFTEN a celebrated taste at the site where Jean-Pierre Roma once settled. As a trader, he imported cocoa from the West Indies to trade with France, Quebec, and Fortress Louisbourg.

At the time, chocolate was a precious commodity and was served to those of the upper classes both in France and in New France. Jean-Pierre Roma was known to have enjoyed chocolate in the form of a hot beverage, as did those living in Fortress Louisbourg.

Chocolate was considered to be medicinal and an aphrodisiac but soon became a coveted beverage by those who could afford the luxury. The addition of eggs and spices was common.

PLAIN CHOCOLATE (PIERRE BLOT)

Here is an historic recipe by French chef Pierre Blot from his book *Practical Cookery for Ladies and Professional Cooks* (1867) followed by a more adaptable version courtesy of Parks Canada.

THE QUANTITY OF chocolate for a certain quantity of milk is according to taste.

Two ounces of chocolate make a good cup of it, and rather thick.

Break the chocolate in pieces, put it in a tin saucepan with a teaspoon of water to an ounce of chocolate, and set it on a rather slow fire.

Stir now and then till thoroughly melted.

While the chocolate is melting, set the quantity of milk desired in another tin saucepan on the fire, and as soon as it rises, and when the chocolate is melted as directed above, turn the milk into the chocolate little by little, beating well at the same time with an egg beater.

Keep beating and boiling after being mixed, for three or four minutes; take off and serve. If both chocolate and milk are good it will be frothy, and no better nutritious drink can be had.

FRENCH HOT CHOCOLATE

Courtesy of Parks Canada

- 1 oz/3 g good quality chocolate bar or ground chocolate
- 1 cup/250 ml water or milk
- 1 tsp/5 g sugar
- Spices and flavourings to taste (cinnamon, nutmeg, cloves, vanilla, orange flower water.)
- Egg yolk (optional)

HEAT LIQUID AND, if using milk, don't let it boil.

Grate chocolate and melt into the liquid.

If you are adding an egg yolk, beat it first with a small amount of the warm liquid, then add the mixture to the pot and beat it in.

Add sugar and a combination of spices to taste.

For best results, prepare the chocolate drink the night before and refrigerate overnight.

Reheat, whipping or frothing the chocolate.

98 MCPHAIL PARK RD.
VERNON BRIDGE, PE

CHAPTER 14

VERNON BRIDGE, PRINCE EDWARD ISLAND

ORWELL CORNER HISTORIC VILLAGE

The Hard Work it takes to put food on the table

DEEP IN THE green, rolling countryside of Prince Edward Island, the sign at Orwell Corner invites visitors to take a turn, and visit a community, as it would have been in 1895. There's a farm and home, a general store stocked to the gills with Victorian goods, a community centre now opened as a teahouse, a church and school, and a shed of farm machinery. The village is alive with activity and the comforting smell of fresh bread baking fills the air. A collection of old photos share with visitors images of those who once lived in this corner of the Island.

The village at Orwell Corner is brought to life by costumed characters, most eager to fill guests' heads with details about how life used to be. Those who wander in can easily get lost for a few hours of bliss in the slow lane of bygone days.

A horse comes out of the barn, harnessed to take visitors on a short wagon ride through the countryside. Young men scythe the grain in the fields. Another swings hay in the barn to feed the animals, stopping to bottle-feed a lamb. Laundry hangs on the line behind the store and folk gather in front of the store to gossip. Inside

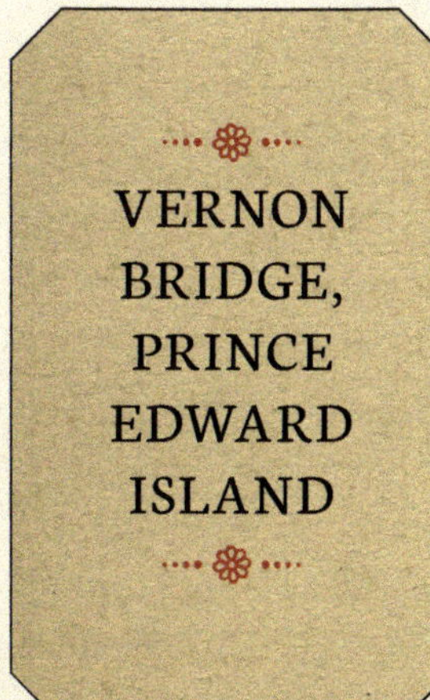

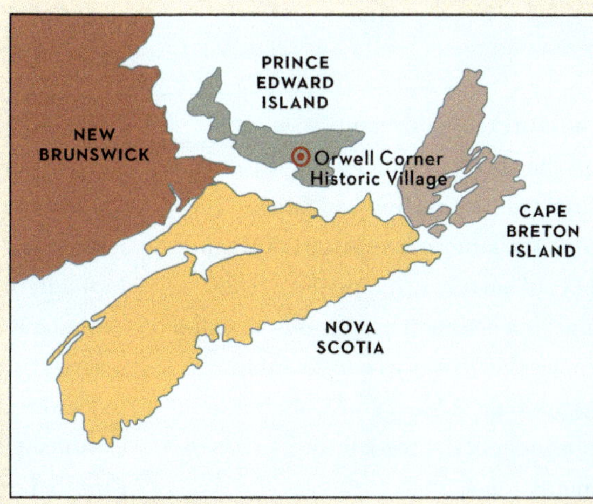

the storekeeper is happy to show off the amazing gadgetry of the day, toys, candy, clothing and fabrics that took the fancy of women back then. Lots of bartering happened in that store, as people traded goods to make each other's lives as comfortable as possible. A blacksmith shop is a reminder of the work it took to create metal items.

Europeans moved to this area in the early 1800's when Captain John MacDonald helped families from the Isle of Skye in Scotland and County Monaghan in Ireland resettle in Canada. Rick and Dennis Clarke arrived from Ireland in 1856, moved to Orwell Corner a few years later and established the General Store. United Empire Loyalists also made this area

their home and many area residents are ancestors of the original settlers.

Experiences of the past are important at Orwell Corner and learning what it takes to feed a family is as important today as it was back then.

Visitors are given the chance to cut grain from the field, grind it into flour and bake a loaf of bread. And when the stomach starts to growl, a taste of the past is waiting at the community centre turned tearoom. Traditional baked goods can be ordered as well as sandwiches on homemade bread. This is where the community once gathered to share food together on festive occasions.

A warm welcome and a chance to experience life at Orwell Corner is shared with all who come "a callin" at Orwell Corner.

PIE, A CHIN WAG AND A SIGH OF RELIEF

Orwell Corner, Prince Edward Island, 1898

MRS. CLARKE WIPED her hands on her apron and looked through the screen to watch her three boys working in the field. They were swinging their scythes to harvest the oats and she admired the strong men they had become.

"Which one would take over the farm after we are too old to continue?" she wondered.

The eldest seemed to love working in the general store the family owned. He was good with people, especially the ladies. The youngest wanted to spend all his time helping the blacksmith and seemed to have a gift for that kind of work.

But Jude seemed to understand how to put food on the table. He knew the farm down into the soil, he could grow any plant, and he knew the animals like they were his friends. He was strong and undaunted by any job he had to learn. Already today, he brought his mother milk that she turned into butter using her hand churn. He collected eggs from the chickens, fed them and moved on to milk the goat and bottle feed the lambs. He understood how every aspect of the farm intertwined with the other. To be sure, the sweet cider they drank in the summer came from his labour. He would rather be home working on the farm than sitting in the classroom any day and seemed to find any excuse to avoid school to learn the farming trade.

Today, Mrs. Clarke planned to bake his favourite with the eggs and apples he brought in for her. She would use her new Jubilee Cook Book, the one with Queen Victoria on the cover, and make Jude's favourite, Apple Meringue Pie. She made a sweet applesauce, blended in four egg yolks, lemon zest and cinnamon to give it a special flavour.

When the screen door slammed, she invited Jude to sit down, have a piece of apple meringue pie and a chinwag.

"Do you think you'd be takin over the farm from me and Pa someday?" she asked in a hopeful voice.

"Been thinkin bout it," he said with all the wisdom of an old man. "Iffen I don't, I'm afeard nobody else will. Won't be none of them brothers of mine. But somebody gotta raise the food that goes on the table and I reckon I'd be good at it."

Mrs. Clarke sighed with relief, gave him a kiss and cut him a second piece of pie.

JUBILE
VALUABLE RECIPES
Personally Tested and Vouched for by
the Ladies whose names appear
under the Recipes

APPLE MERINGUE PIE

From the *Jubilee Cookbook* by the Ladies' Aid Society of the Methodist Church, Charlottetown, PEI

- 1 quart applesauce
- 1 cup sugar
- 1 Tbsp butter
- 1 tsp cinnamon
- pinch salt
- essence of lemon
- 4 Eggs
- 4 Tbsp powdered sugar

TO A QUART of nice applesauce put a cup of white sugar, a tablespoon of butter, a teaspoon of cinnamon, pinch of salt, little essence of lemon.

Beat the yolks of four eggs light; and add to applesauce. Fill the crusts and bake a light brown - no upper crust - then cover with meringue of the four eggs with four tablespoons of powdered sugar.

Sift a little powder on the top and brown lightly. Peach pies made in this way are delicious.

Mrs. Richard Johnson

1907
CHATEAU ALBERT

5 RUE DU PONT
BERTRAND, NB

CHAPTER 15

CARAQUET, NEW BRUNSWICK

VILLAGE HISTORIQUE ACADIEN

"To be Acadian is to have pardon in your heart and to look forward with hope."
-Zachary Richard

THE HISTORY OF Acadians on Canada's east coast is a story of strength, and modern-day visitors to the Village Historique Acadien in northern New Brunswick can experience this with their own eyes. Acadians were some of the earliest settlers from France to inhabit what are now Nova Scotia, New Brunswick and Prince Edward Island. In 1755, during land disputes between the French and British, the Acadians were driven off their land by the British. Some were deported back to France while others resettled along the eastern seaboard and as far away as the southern States. The Cajun culture in New Orleans is an example of Acadian influence.

Visitors to this recreated Acadian village are invited to walk slowly and experience Acadian life as it existed in this area between 1770 and 1949. The forty buildings along a winding two-kilometre path include farms, homes, a gristmill, workshops, businesses, two general stores, a chapel, a school and an old gas station beside a hotel—and all the doors are open.

Buildings in the village have been moved from the surrounding area or authentically rebuilt. Visitors can

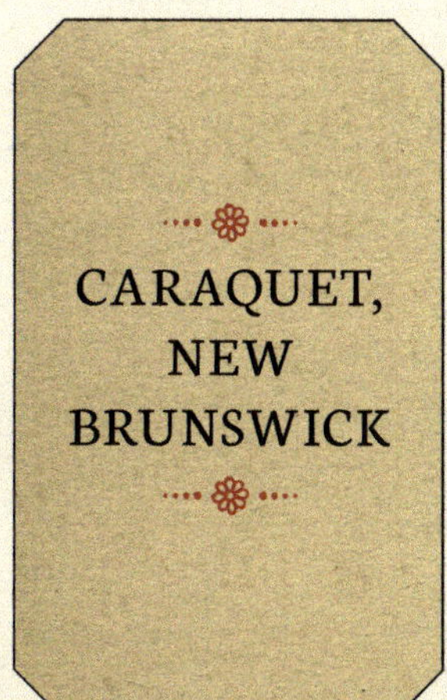

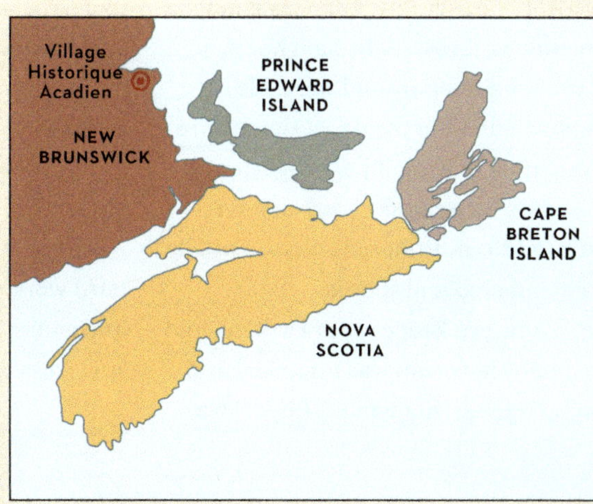

watch how settlers gardened, raised animals, forged metal, ground grain, printed newspapers and worked at all the other crafts and trades necessary for self-sufficient lives. Interesting costumed characters going about their daily lives take time to chat and answer questions in both French and English. The resourceful and industrious Acadians were known to live well off the land and sea, and learned to adapt wherever they settled, even when conditions were difficult.

In the earliest log cabin dating back to 1773, Mr. Martin cooks a simple meal in a cast iron pot over the open-hearth fireplace while he talks about his life.

In the Godin home, where it is still 1890, Madame prepares Fricotte à la truite with potatoes and onions and an apple pie using dried apples to be served for the noon dîner. At another home, the smell of fresh baking bread draws guests to an outdoor oven. Visitors can see how kitchens changed as time progressed. In each home, families gather around the table to enjoy their noon meal together before returning to work. Long-forgotten Acadian cooking skills are demonstrated so traditions of the past will be remembered and shared.

A tavern keeper pours a drink and explains how rum was imported and how bagosse (homemade liquor) was made using the same ingredients that made the bread of the time. One of several eateries, The Table des Ancêtres, invites diners into the old Dugas home to sample traditional Acadian tastes. Beans, soups, homemade bread with molasses, biscuits, and blueberry cake are some of the many offerings of the day. Acadians were known for living with a sense of fun and named their dishes to give a chuckle. By-the-door Soup was given this name because the vegetable garden was next to the house.

As visitors turn the corner so too does time, into the twentieth century when horses traveled beside cars and an old Irving station pumps gas for a Model T Ford that sputters around the village.

At the end of the walkway is the Château Albert, originally a hotel built in 1907 that burned down in Caraquet in 1955. A replica of the hotel, rebuilt in the Village Historique Acadien using the original plans, opened in 2000. Some guests spend the night as they would have in the 1920s, dine in the restaurant and wake up in the morning to share another day in the life of the Acadian families of the village.

These were lives well lived, through hard work, a strong sense of family and enduring cultural pride that survives to this day.

THE BIRTHDAY DINÊR

Caraquet, New Brunswick, 1870

FALL HAD FINALLY kissed goodbye the last days of summer on the Dugas farm and harvest was in full swing. It was frosty and cold and Veronique's hands were numb as she dug potatoes from the mud. Once in the warm house she emptied the harvest from her apron onto the wooden table.

A voice from the corner spoke out. "Ah, the smell of fresh potatoes from the ground."

"Now how can you tell these are potatoes when you can't even see, Suzanne?" asked Veronique.

"I smell the earth, and even though I am blind, my nose knows potatoes. Now hand them over when they are ready to grate."

Veronique was making the family's favourite, Rappie Pie, for Suzanne's birthday. Suzanne, Veronique's sister, had lived with the family for years. Family was everything to this generous, proud Acadian family and she was part of them.

Veronique cubed the pork and fried it with onions on the stove, while she peeled potatoes and handed them to Suzanne to grate. Other potatoes were boiled to be mashed. In a large bowl the mashed and grated potatoes were combined with meat, onions, eggs, pepper, summer savory and coriander and Veronique mixed it all with her hands.

Pouring the mixture into a baking pan she sprinkled pork fat over the dish and placed it in the oven. It would be ready just in time for the rest of the family returning home for dîner at noon.

Just as the clock chimed for the twelfth time, Germain and the children came in from their chores and the Rappie Pie came out of the oven.

"Happy Birthday, Auntie Suzanne" each said, as they hugged her tight.

"We must have walked miles in the fields today," said the smallest Dugas child.

On every birthday, Suzanne enjoyed telling a story. It was important to her to keep the traditions of her people alive. Once all the plates were filled and they had thanked the Lord, Suzanne began.

"I heard you say you walked far today, my petite cher, but you would not be enjoying this dîner, in this home, on this land if it weren't for a very brave and famous man who lived close by before us and took a very long walk. A five hundred mile walk." The children were speechless.

"Let us clap for a man named François Gionet who lived here many years ago. Your grandfather was his friend and told me about his long walk.

François walked from our town of Caraquet all the way to Halifax to get the land grants for our Acadian forefathers. It was after the time when many Acadians were driven away from their land and lost everything to the British. So now, because François made the long walk we can look out over the land and know that it is ours. And we can plant our potatoes and eat our Rappie Pie with our family in peace and happiness."

Germain pulled out his fiddle and they began to sing one of their favourite songs. Veronique slipped away from the table and brought back Suzanne's sweet. She held it under her nose so she could smell the vapors of molasses and cinnamon.

"Now let's nibble on the Nun's Fingers," said Veronique as she put down a plate of long finger-like pieces of bread and a dipping bowl of molasses. They laughed heartily at the silly name of the treats.

The family who loved to work and eat and sing together finished their feast, and it was a long time before anyone complained of long walks again.

RAPPIE PIE

Both recipes from: *A Taste of Acadie* with permission of Marielle Cormier-Boudrea.

- 2 lbs (1kg) fatty pork
- 2 onions, chopped
- 12 large potatoes, grated very fine
- 4 large potatoes, boiled and mashed
- 2 eggs
- 1 Tbsp(15 ml) salt, pepper, summer savory, coriander
- ¼ lb (125 g) pork fat
- ½ lb (250 g) fried salt pork

THERE ARE MANY *methods of cooking Rappie Pie and here is one.*

Cut the pork into cubes and sauté them in a frying pan. Add the onions and sauté until golden brown. Set the meat and onions aside.

Grate the raw potatoes and extract any water from the potatoes by putting them into a cotton bag and squeezing vigorously. (The potatoes may first be rinsed in cold water to remove their starchy pink colour.)

Place the mashed potatoes in a large bowl with the meat, onions, grated potatoes, eggs, salt, pepper, summer savory and coriander, and combine them thoroughly.

Place the pork fat in an 8" by 15" (20 cm x 35 cm) casserole dish and pour the potato mixture over the pork fat. Sprinkle with the pieces of fried salt pork.

Bake at 350°F/180°C for at least 2 hours or until the top is golden brown.

NUN'S FINGERS

USE DOUGH LEFT OVER from baking bread. Cut into small pieces and roll them into finger shapes. Deep fry the fingers like doughnuts. Serve with molasses.

5804 ROUTE 102
PRINCE WILLIAM, NB

CHAPTER 16

PRINCE WILLIAM, NEW BRUNSWICK

KINGS LANDING HISTORICAL SETTLEMENT

"Getting here is easy, leaving is the hard part."

ALONG THE ST. JOHN'S RIVER, close to Prince William, New Brunswick, is a small community alive with activity. Farmers feed cattle, women hang laundry to dry in the wind, gardeners are picking fresh vegetables from the garden and well-fed people leave the front door of the King's Head Inn. In many ways, it is not too different from life today, with one difference. Kings Landing is a living history museum showing life as it was for those who settled in the area from 1820 to 1920. Most emigrated from the British Isles so a rich cultural mix of English, Irish and Scottish cultures can be seen in the settlement. Mi'kmaq and Maliseet First Nations inhabited the area for centuries before the European settlers arrived.

Many historic buildings were preserved when moved, or reconstructed on the 300-acre site when the Mactaquac Dam was built in the 1960s. The historical settlement now consists of 70 period buildings where costumed interpreters show visitors how settlers grew and prepared their food, raised livestock and went about life at that time. The village shows the importance of hard work and self-sufficiency back in those times.

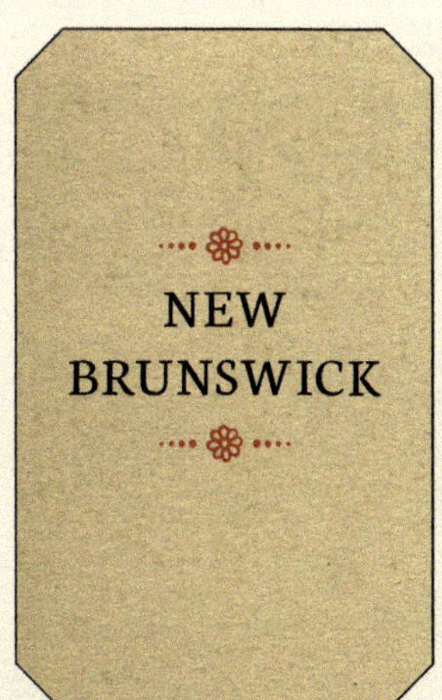

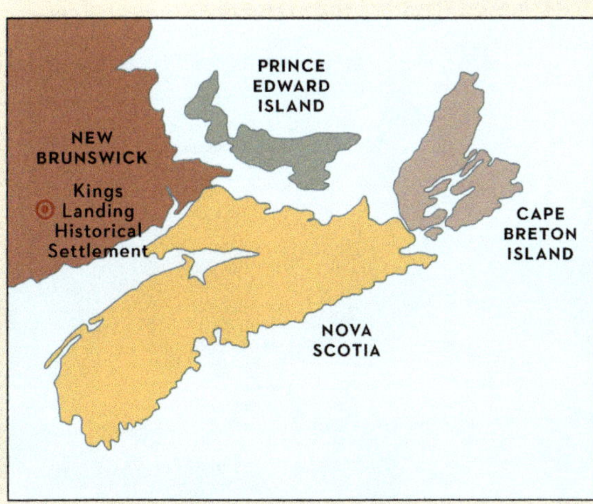

As visitors stroll through the village they are drawn into the homes by the smell of home cooking. Homes from different eras show progress through the years, and how cooking became easier with time. Leaning on the railing of the general store, a group of musicians might entertain a small crowd with lively music. No motors can be heard as the farmers work the fields. Children can pet the lambs and watch a cow being milked.

A farmer might ask visitors to help pick vegetables from the garden or his wife might show how to mix gingerbread in the farmhouse. Children can sit at desks in the schoolhouse. Two churches are part of the settlement representing a time when most members of communities gathered to worship and socialize together. The general store shelves are stocked with interesting goods from the past to purchase. Tasting the old-fashioned candy delights children.

At noon, strolling through the homes, visitors may see a farming family sharing a dinner from a time when a hearty meal was needed for the strength to labour all afternoon. Visitors can enjoy a meal at the King's Head Inn, where food is served by women dressed as they would have in the 1800s. The Inn represents life as it would have been for settlers who needed a meal or a place to sleep overnight while on their travels.

Kings Landing presents themed weekends during the year, allowing visitors to learn about a specific aspect of life through hands-on activities. It is possible to watch how the food was harvested and prepared for different seasons.

Walking away from Kings Landing leaves a visitor with a feeling of wanting to come back soon, to live life in the past with their new friends from the settlement. They have a saying at the settlement: "Getting here is easy, leaving is the hard part."

HEAVEN IS IN THE KITCHEN AT THE HOLYOAKE HOME

Orwell Corner, Prince Edward Island, 1898

I REMEMBER THE day Grampie told me to fetch the horses, we was headin on a trip. It were a cold day and the leaves had all turned to gold.

"You're old enough little sprout, to learn how to make a living from what we grow here on the land. It's 1855, you are what, eight now?"

"Nine, Grampie." He was getting a little forgetful.

My attention wandered as I watched Grampie load the apples and pumpkins onto the wagon and hitch up the horses. I had never been on a trip overnight and this was to be a real adventure. Mama packed us lunches and told us to be careful.

We rode for hours across the countryside and I could see no place where Grampie could sell the fruits of our land. Occasionally we would pass a farm and wave to those in the fields. After a while we stopped to water the horses and have some of Mama's lunch of turkey sandwiches and fresh apples from the buggy. Off in the distance I could see a large house.

"There she is," said Grampie with relief in his voice. I could tell he was tired.

"It's the Holyoakes' place, and this here's where we'll stay the night."

I had never seen a house with a sign over the door and this one had a King's head on it. I had heard tell that this is where travellers could stay.

I remember feeling the warmth from the big stone fireplace as we walked through the front door. It was noisy with voices, and I had never seen so many strangers in one place.

Mrs. Holyoake wiped her hands on her apron and came over to greet Grampie.

"Just in time, Charlie. I have just run out of pumpkins and people is screamin for my pumpkin pie."

"Wait till you taste the food in this place," said Grampie, to make her smile.

He had just introduced me to this friendly woman in the apron when she grabbed my hand and took me into the kitchen to taste some cookies. I had never seen a kitchen like it in all my life. So many different kinds of food being cooked all at once.

"You must be busy cooking for all these men," I said shyly.

"They'll get what they get," she said, "and I'm sure glad you brought me those pumpkins and apples. We're having Tipsy Cake tonight, cuz there was no apples left in the cold room for pie." She pushed a plate my way with a piece of gingerbread covered in whipped cream. I remember thinking I were in heaven.

I asked her what Tipsy Cake was, and she told me it would be a surprise, but it was my Grampie's favourite.

How did she know? The twinkle in her eye made me wonder. She told me I could help her and that was a special moment because Mama never let me help in the kitchen, being a boy.

She set a cake on the table and told me that she had cut it in the shape of a hedgehog and now we would make it prickly. I loved hedgehogs. From a big bowl of sliced almonds she showed me how to stick them on end in the cake. That kept me busy for a while. When we were done, she poured somethin over the cake. It smelled like Grampie's breath sometimes after he'd been tippin his cup.

"Shhhhh," she said, and put her finger over her lips. "We'll add some creamy custard just before it is time to serve."

That night we shared a delicious dinner of venison roast, vegetables and wonderful soft rolls with all the other travellers at a big table. Mrs. Holyoake came through the kitchen door smiling and placed the Tipsy Cake right in front of Grampie. He beamed.

And I beamed along with him, knowing I had helped make the cake that made Grampie so happy.

TIPSY CAKE

Courtesy of From the Kitchens of Kings Landing

BAKE A SPONGE cake and cut in the shape of a hedgehog. Blanch sweet almonds, remove the skins and cut them into long strips as nearly of a size as possible. Roast the sliced almonds, stirring frequently for a few minutes in the oven, then stick them regularly into the cake. Set it in a deep dish, and then at least twelve hours before it is required, sprinkle over it a quarter cup of sherry wine or brandy or, if this is too expensive, use raisin wine.

Make a custard sauce or soft custard, and, shortly before serving, pour it cold round the base of the cake.

A tipsy cake is British in origin. The old recipes would have come with settlers from England.

GINGERBREAD

Gingerbread recipe shared from the Kitchens of Kings Landing

- ½ cup butter
- 1 cup molasses
- ½ cup brown sugar
- 1 Tbsp ginger
- ½ tsp cloves
- ½ tsp cinnamon
- 2 cups or more flour
- 1 tsp soda
- 1 Tbsp sour milk or buttermilk

CUT UP HALF a cup of butter into a cup of molasses which has been warmed slightly to melt the butter. Add brown sugar by degrees to the molasses and butter; then stir in one tablespoon ginger, ½ teaspoon cloves and ½ teaspoon of cinnamon. Add gradually sufficient flour to make a dough stiff (approximately 2 cups enough to roll out easily); and lastly, a small teaspoon of soda dissolved in a tablespoon of sour milk or buttermilk.

Mix and stir the stiff dough well with a wooden spoon, but do not knead it; roll out the dough into a sheet half an inch thick, and cut it into round flat cakes with a tin cutter, with the edge of a tumbler, or cut into shapes like gingerbread men.

Bake them in a brisk oven (350°F to 375°F) about 8 minutes, taking care that they do not burn. Gingerbread scorches sooner than any other cake. These are very crisp and will keep a long time in a covered tin.

DIVISION NO. 9, SUBD D
L'ANSE AUX MEADOWS, NL

CHAPTER 17

L'ANSE AUX MEADOWS, NEWFOUNDLAND

L'ANSE AUX MEADOWS NATIONAL HISTORIC SITE

A Viking settlement

A WALK ACROSS the boggy land towards a sod longhouse is a walk back to the year 1000. L'Anse Aux Meadows is located on the north coast of Newfoundland close to St. Anthony, making the journey a long trip for visitors but well worth the effort. In this cold and barren land, icebergs drift by from the north much of the year. It is hard to imagine how the Norse or those we call Vikings were blown in their ships to this corner of the earth.

L'Anse Aux Meadows has been declared a UNESCO World Heritage site and is the only authenticated Viking settlement in North America. A sod-roofed longhouse and two other buildings have been re-constructed so visitors can learn of the life of the Vikings. It is believed that the first European contact was made with the indigenous peoples of this land some five hundred years before Christopher Columbus landed on this continent.

Visitors are met by characters realistically reenacting the parts of Viking characters and carrying on with daily life in and around the longhouse. Ragnar, the blacksmith, makes nails for the ships from bog iron he collected on the land. Inside

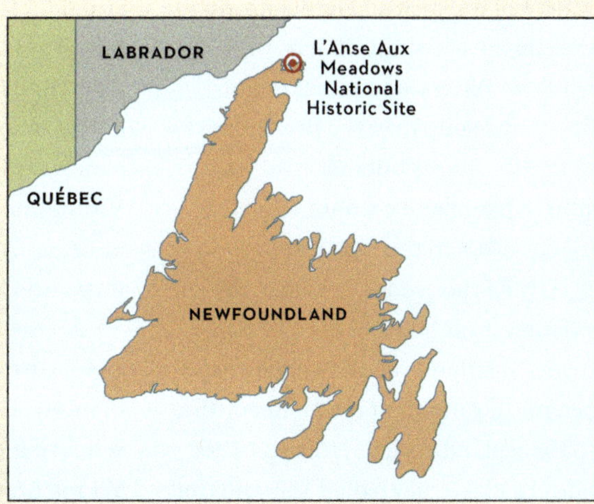

the longhouse, the fires are the only source of warmth and light. The delicate music of the tagelharpa plays, while a Viking woman makes flatbread and soup over the fire. Bjorn the Beautiful shares tales with all who stop to listen and a woman quietly weaves wool in the next room.

Over a thousand years ago, the wooden trade ships of the Vikings from Greenland set off to explore the oceans beyond their lands. According to the Icelandic sagas left to us, they found a place they called Vinland that gifted them with wild grapes, treasured for the production of wine, and butternut trees that were a coveted wood and food product. The location of this place called Vinland remains a mystery but we do know that the Vikings had a temporary settlement at L'Anse Aux Meadows to repair their boats and act as a base for exploration.

Archeological digs began in the 1960s after locals noticed the mounds of interest. Digging has unearthed relics that confirm that the site was Viking from around the year 1000.

Metal objects and a spindle used to make wool show that both men and women temporarily occupied the site. The local indigenous peoples also inhabited these lands both before and long after the Vikings left.

Visitors are curious about what the Vikings ate while they lived on this land. Bones of sea mammals have been found in the archeological digs, and it is easy to speculate that they hunted game and birds. Although the Norse grew grains and vegetables in other countries, there is no evidence they planted gardens in this cold, barren land. Some food may have been brought in their trading ships, but they used what they could from the land and sea.

At L'Anse Aux Meadows, there are echoes of a time when the Mighty Norse wandered the world.

They whisper to us of their travels through the found traces of their life, and their spirits still trudge the windy landscape.

FINDING FOOD WHERE THE WINDS CARRY US

RAGNAR PUSHED OPEN the heavy wooden door of the longhouse, and felt the warmth of the fire and the smell of food cooking. He had been on the damp land all day collecting small pieces of a stone known as bog iron and hauling them back to smelt into iron in his forge.

Helga had also worked all day collecting lyme grass that she would dry to turn into grain to make flat-bread. She was running low on the barley they brought when they left on this sea journey from their colony in Greonland (Greenland).

But there were many mouths to feed and she was always worried about their next meal. Supplies were getting low as winter turned into spring. They could fish and some smoked seal meat hung in the rafters. It had been a while since a deer had been hunted and brought back to the longhouse to provide a good feed of venison.

"Didn't think we'd be gone from home this long," she said to Ragnar, the worry showing in her face.

"We sail with the wind, and where the stars lead us, and we cannot know these things," replied Ragnar. "The ships need repair and we need to replace the rusty nails before we head back," he said firmly.

They had recently returned from sailing further south in their large boat to Vinland, and the journey had been a rough one. They would return to Grœnland with wood from the butternut tree and grapes, both highly treasured goods. The large woolen sails had worn through in several places and Ana was working to spin the wool they'd brought along so she could repair them. Ragnar would work his iron magic to make the many nails that would be needed to reinforce their ship to carry them back to Greenland.

"Now what do you have to feed me for my evening nattmal?" He hadn't eaten since morning.

He sat down on a bench built into the walls of the wooden longhouse and looked around in the faint light. Old Bjorn was telling a story to a young one, and he began to play his instrument, creating a haunting music against the backdrop of the howling wind outside. Ana was in the next room quietly working her wonders with the wool. The fire warmed his cold hands and dried off his damp woolen clothing. The others would start arriving for their evening meal soon. Ragnar watched his wife Helgar as she cooked his meal. They had some grain left from the journey but needed to depend more on making flour from lyme grass collected along the shore. It then had to be dried and ground into flour and as long as supplies lasted, Helga would add a bit of barley flour brought with them to add texture and taste to her flatbread. She added just enough of the water she had collected from the stream earlier to form the mixture into a dough. With her cold hands, she formed small balls and kneaded them on a piece of rock. She knew when they were ready to pat into flat shapes and put them on a hot cast iron pan. She took a moment to stir the hearty soup of smoked cod, rutabaga and some old withered carrots that were aging quickly in the bins. Her knowledge of how to add wild herbs gave the soup a rich taste of the earth. As she spooned a bowl of soup for Ragnar, she flipped the flat bread over and handed it to him. "Eat it while it is hot, or you will eat a rock."

Ragnar was warmed by the soup, and he knew he was fortunate to have Helga to share his journey to Vinland.

Their faces were lit by the fire and they looked content, even if just for the moment. For them, life was lived for the day.

VIKING FLAT BREAD

Here is a recipe (a Viking woman would never measure amounts), that describes one version of flatbread. The taste would vary depending on the types of flour that were tossed into the wooden bowl.

- 2½ cups of wheat flour (taste is similar to lyme grass)
- ½ cup rye flour
- ½ cup barley flour
- 2 cups or a bit less liquid (water)
- 2 tsp salt

MIX ALL INGREDIENTS and knead together. Roll into balls and flatten each one. Place on a hot griddle to bake and flip over.

Best eaten warm before they become too hard.

L'Anse aux Meadows was a stopover for the Vikings visiting Vinland and there is no evidence that crops of grains were planted. Stores of barley were likely carried in their trade ships. They also collected lyme grass, a grain that was widely used in Iceland, and Greenland and grew on the coastal areas of Newfoundland. The flour from lyme grass was more difficult to process but tasted similar to wheat flour.

VIKING SOUP

Author's interpretation of how soup was made.

- 6 cups water
- meat/fish
- foraged green vegetables (dandelion or nettle leaves, wild caraway, wild garlic, wild mustard)
- salt

PUT A POT on the stove and add 6 cups of water. Add a piece of meat, or fish to the pot and let it boil for a while to create a broth. Remove the meat or fish and break into pieces, adding it back to the broth. Add any foraged greens or vegetables available.

On the north coast of Newfoundland over seventy edible wilds grow, some of which they would have used to add to soups. Wilds like dandelion leaves, nettle leaves, wild caraway, wild garlic, mustard and many more. Salt would have been added to taste.

1 POOL AVE.
FERRYLAND, NL

CHAPTER 18

FERRYLAND, NEWFOUNDLAND

COLONY OF AVALON NATIONAL HISTORIC SITE

An Early British Colony with a Touch of Class

A WALK ON a cobblestone street on a rugged peninsula that stretches out into the sea takes visitors back to the 1600s in the National Historic Site of the Colony of Avalon. The smell of food cooking and wood smoke wafts through the fresh sea air. Visitors become history sleuths as they visit the stone ruins of what was a thriving English fishing and trading colony - with a difference. Its foundations and over two million artifacts that have been dug from the rocky earth tell the story of a settlement with touches of surprising sophistication.

A guided walking tour brings the colony alive as the guide describes life in the Colony, using artists' renditions of the buildings to help recall what it would have looked like. The original cobblestone street, reminiscent of the English homeland, remains today, and was once lined with stone and timber houses. For thirty years, archeologists and volunteer visitors have been digging to uncover the well preserved foundations of a bakery/brewhouse, a warehouse for storing traded goods, a forge, the original well and sea wall and even a sea flushed privy. The Gentleman's Garden of showy flowers and the Kitchen Garden have

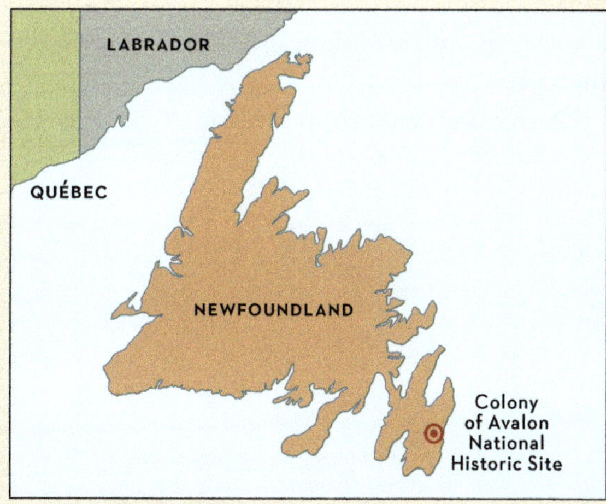

been recreated using historical data gleaned from letters to England from the Colony.

Settlers from England first arrived in 1621, although the waters in the area had been fished for many years. The colony was most prosperous during the latter half of the 17th century. David Kirke, Newfoundland's first governor, arrived in Newfoundland in 1638. He died in 1654 while imprisoned in England for tax evasion. After David was imprisoned, his wife, Sarah Kirke, managed the colony (renamed the Pool Plantation) until her death in 1683. Her business became highly successful. She sent ships of saltfish to Mediterranean and Iberian ports, then purchased wine, olive oil, fruit and other goods to sell at English and Dutch ports bringing labour and supplies back to Newfoundland. A community existed there for many years but with time, changed, as inhabitants moved away. Now the archeological digs continue to unlock the past.

Beyond the door of a present day building lies a kitchen that looks and feels like it could have been there in 1621. There is often a surprise cooking demonstration in the open-hearth fireplace such as a carrett (carrot) pudding or a sallett (salad) of hen, explaining the wonderful smells that drift outside. Here were served not simple fish and bread recipes but rather, something quite fancy.

Receipts (recipes) travelled from England in favourite books and in the memories of colonists.

Today, a long table with benches invites visitors to settle in and learn about dishes that might have been cooked at the colony.

In the summer, the innovative Great Colonial Cook Off program is run from the kitchen and online, sharing historic recipes and inviting enthusiasts from around the world to try cooking history at home. The Colony of Avalon continues to grow its knowledge by the day as the archeological digs continue to unravel the mysteries of a small piece of England that once existed on Newfoundland's rugged coast.

EXQUISITE TASTE ON THE RUGGED COAST

Colony of Avalon, Newfoundland - Early winter 1665

MARY SET THE plate down on the finely set breakfast table in front of lady Sarah Kirke and watched for her smile. This was a different breakfast from the one she served day in, day out.

"Oh, so exquisite, and you remembered that receipt," commented Sarah when Mary delivered her special surprise.

Mary started work that day before sunrise. The first snow of the winter had fallen during the night and she pulled up her wool scarf to keep out the chill from the ocean winds. She slid along the icy cobblestone street and for a moment she felt she could have been back in England. The brewhouse was her first stop to get beere and barm to make her manchet, (a type of bread) for the Kirke household.

Mary looked up to see the sun shining through the falling snow. It reminded her of a dish called Eggs Into Snow. Mrs. Kirke had brought several receipt books with her from England and would often read them to Mary by the fireside. Unable to read, Mary learned the receipts by listening carefully and trusting her memory. Now, she remembered how to make Eggs Into Snow from the French book by Varenne. She stopped to collect eggs and was chilled by the time she returned to the warm kitchen.

She added some wood to the grand fireplace, pulled on her linen apron and started her special breakfast. As she broke the eggs, she separated the whites and beat them with her birch twig whisk until they were soft and fluffy. On a buttered dish she made a rounded nest shape with the whites and gently set them in the coals to brown lightly. She added the yolks in the middle to cook, then set it on the most lovely plate she could find.

Sarah was fond of Mary, her servant and cook, and together they travelled by ship from England. Mary felt fortunate to work for such a wealthy and influential woman. She knew that while she baked fine white manchet for her lady, those less fortunate were making their bread by grinding dried peas and beans and using coarsely ground flours.

She remembered well the taste of that bread from her childhood in England.

Each day the fishing boats returned with their catch in the late morning, and Mary knew just the right time to walk down to the docks to pick the best fish for tonight's dinner of Will Seethed Fish.

She swept the snow off the herbs in the garden and picked sage, parsley and thyme. With the beere she brought from the brewhouse, she poached the fish, adding water, a spoonful of butter and the herbs. The fish poached over the fire to perfection. After dinner, Sarah and Mary sat by the fire.

"Let's bring out that French book of cookery and read about some more tasty creations," said Sarah. "We will put elegance on the tables in this corner of our Newfoundland coast."

EGGS INTO SNOW

The French Cook - Francois Pierre La Varenne 1651

- eggs
- butter
- salt
- rosewater

BREAK SOME EGGS, sever the whites from the yolks; put the yolks in a dish upon butter, and season them with salt, and set them upon hot cinders. Beat and whip well the whites, and a little before you serve, powre (pour) them on the yolks with a drop of rosewater, and the fire-shovels over them, then sugar and serve.

This is a recipe such as may have been made in the Colony of Avalon. Eggs were plentiful and this early book of recipes inspired a sophisticated way to serve the humble egg.

WILL SEETHED COD

Original Recipe by Thomas Dawson from *The Good Huswifes Handmaide for the Kitchin* Published in 1594

Here is another recipe that might have been cooked at the Colony of Avalon in the 1700s. A modern version for today's cook courtesy of Colony of Avalon.

- 2 lbs fish fillets
- 2 Tbsp butter
- 2 cups beer
- 1 tsp salt
- Freshly ground pepper
- ½ cup parsley
- 1 Tbsp thyme
- ½ tsp rosemary
- ¼ cup white vinegar

PLACE THE FISH in a heavy skillet. Add the butter and cover with the beer.

Simmer for several minutes, then add the salt, pepper to taste, parsley, thyme and rosemary.

Simmer an additional 15 minutes or until the fish is tender and flakes easily.

Add the vinegar and heat briefly.

Arrange the fish on a serving dish and cover with the broth.

To seeth Fresh Fish. Take a little water, and as much Beere and salt, and put therto Parsley, Time and Rosemarie, and let all these boyle togeathere. Then put in your Salmon, and make your broth Sharpe with some Vinigre.

83 FISHER ST.
PORT AU CHOIX, NL

CHAPTER 19

PORT AU CHOIX, NEWFOUNDLAND

FRENCH ROOMS BREAD OVEN

Where French Fishermen Made Bread

ON THE NORTHERN peninsula of Newfoundland is a breathtaking oceanside drive called the Viking Trail. A turn towards the town of Port au Choix leads travellers to a thriving fishing community with a colourful history. The French Rooms Cultural Centre and Bread Oven extend a warm invitation to visit the local traditional French Oven. Visitors can watch bread being baked as it was by the migratory French fishermen who fished these waters for over 400 years.

Guests are served warm baked rolls, local preserves and a cup of tea delivered by characters in French period costume, and learn about the fishing history of the area. In the dome-shaped brick oven a fire is set early in the day and by two in the afternoon, the buns are ready, a delicious reminder of how French cookery has woven its way into today's cuisine.

In 1713, the French were given rights by the British to fish off the coast of Newfoundland, but were not allowed to form settlements.

Port au Choix was an important harbour at that time and the French used the land only to salt and prepare their fish for the journey back to Europe. There were many Roman Catholic religious holidays all over Europe requiring meatless meals, so

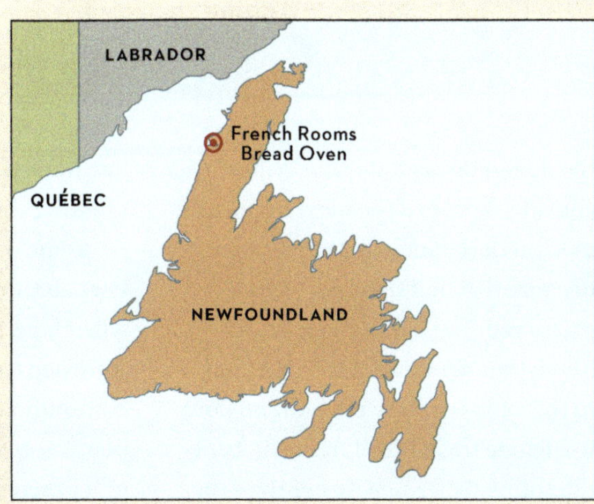

the demand was high. The "salter" was considered one of the most important men on the schooners from France because fish had to be perfectly preserved. The baker was also an important person aboard ship, and in the 1800s ovens were built on land to include fresh bread in the diets of the young fishermen rather than the hardtack they were fed on the journey crossing the ocean.

Some of the earliest settlers of Port au Choix were French fishermen who chose to desert when the ships returned to France. They joined the community of English and Indigenous peoples, but could not speak French or let their ancestry be known. Those

French fishermen are ancestors of some of today's residents in Port au Choix (Port of Choice,) who are now proud to celebrate their French heritage.

In 2004, in celebration of the French presence in Newfoundland, replica outdoor bread ovens were constructed around the coast of the province. Quinpon, La Malouin, Coachman's Cove, Shoe Cove, Boutte du Cap, Port au Choix and Cape St. George all have ovens built by local heritage committees.

What better way to share the French fishing history with visitors than to share a taste and listen to tales of the past.

FOR THE LOVE OF FRESH FRENCH BREAD

Port Aux Choix, Newfoundland 1820

PIERRE PULLED THE first bread loaves out of his new oven that day and the smile on the faces of the fishermen as they stood around waiting, was a sight he would never forget.

Back in France his father had taught him the skill of building an oven and his grandmother was his teacher for the bread making techniques needed to make a perfect loaf. For years he worked in the family bakery, hauling bags of flour and kneading the massive balls of dough. People lined up in the street to buy their bread.

When he learned that the fishing fleet needed a baker, he made the choice to sail to far-off waters. The loss to his family was difficult but he explained with great passion that he would be of better service to the hungry fishermen that provide families in France with the fish they needed to eat on their many religious holidays. To gain permission he told his family stories of the maggot-filled hard tack that the men ate on their journeys across the seas. It worked, and soon he was off to join the fishing fleet with their blessings.

Many a day, he missed the routine and security of his family life at the bakery, most of all when the seas were rough. He cooked no matter how sick he felt.

When they reached land, Pierre spent many days hauling the handmade clay bricks brought by ship from France, carrying them to a level spot above the beach. After building a square base, he topped it with the domed "chapel" (baking chamber), and covered it all with clay. He was proud of the results; his bread stove was a thing of beauty.

Pierre spent many days chopping alder and birch trees for firewood. He carried flour from the ship and began to make the dough, and form the loaves. He made a fire, and when the wood burned down and the bricks turned white, he removed the ashes. It was time to bake.

Pierre noticed that now every fisherman wanted to be his best friend but he made sure that loaves were given out fairly. They could not get enough of the fresh bread and he was busy every minute of every day.

Pierre did not return to France on the ship when it left at the end of the fishing season. In fact, he never left the land by his bread oven.

In the bakery, Port Aux Choix, 1985 . . .

"They called him a deserter," said Brigitte as she talked to a group of local women about her great grandfather, as they ate sweet buns and tea.

"He didn't return to France with the ships, and where do you think he hid?'

The women's imaginations were hard at work.

"He hid under a pile of logs at Mr. Butts' house. When he climbed out the next morning he nearly scared Mr. Butts half to death. He had to cover

his French accent so he would not be discovered. He married and had children and they had children and here I am today. And if I was not, you would not be enjoying the wonderful bread and buns that you eat in my bakeshop."

Brigitte was known for her bread in the town of Port Aux Choix.

Over the years, as she aged, the story changed and she had a twinkle in her eye when she told of the romance of her great-grandfather.

But she did know that it came naturally when she put her hands in the dough to knead–it felt like what she was put on this earth to do.

And she thanked her great grandfather Pierre for that gift.

DOT'S ROLLS

(Recipe used at Dot's Bakery in Port Au Choix) for the buns baked at the French Ovens today. Courtesy of Carolyn Lavers

- 3 lbs, 5 oz flour
- ¼ cup of yeast
- 1 Tbsp salt
- 2 oz sugar
- 2 oz of shortening
- 2 eggs, beat up a bit

MIX LIKE ANY other bread recipe, knead, let rise, knead, let rise and bake for 15 minutes in a 375°F oven until browned on the top.

Makes 3 - 4 dozen of the best buns you have ever tasted.

PHOTO BY Ju Lianna on Unsplash

AUDREY

CHAPTER 20

BATTLE HARBOUR, LABRADOR

BATTLE HARBOUR NATIONAL HISTORIC DISTRICT

Where fishermen gathered

AFTER A NINE-MILE journey across the windy Atlantic waters from Mary's Harbour, the boat lands on the rugged island at the settlement of Battle Harbour. Once off the boat, signs of modern life disappear. Walking where fishermen lived and hearing the stories of Battle Harbour creates a living story in the minds of all who visit. This is a destination for the adventurous, for those willing to travel and stay for a taste of a different time and a way of life.

The wooden buildings of the old fishing community are settled on a hill beside the protected waters of the long strait between islands, called a tickle. The island began as a fishing outpost in the 1770s, and was settled mainly by British fishermen, their families and merchants. The ocean here was rich in cod, salmon, herring and seal, and by the mid 1800s hundreds of fishing and trading schooners from many countries jammed the harbour in the summers. Fish was an important commodity in Europe at that time.

The Trunk system of trade held the fishing locals in a position of constant debt to the merchants, as goods needed for the summer

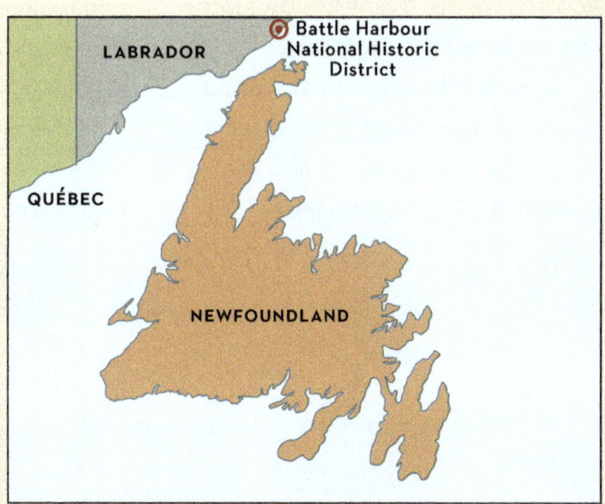

were given in advance and the fishermen could seldom pay back in the required amounts of fish. Families depended mainly on imports from the merchants for most of their needs. The unfair trunk system ended in the 1930s.

In 1893, Dr. Grenfell built a Mission Hospital to serve the fishermen of the outports. The hospital burned in 1930, causing many in the community to move inland during the winter and out to the headland from spring to fall. Battle Harbour was a stopover for Robert Peary who announced his news of reaching the North Pole to the waiting world in 1909. Battle Harbour was abandoned as a community in the 1960s with the Government resettlement plan. After the cod moratorium in 1992, the site was handed over to the Battle Harbour Historic Trust and from 1992 - 1996, work began to rebuild twenty-two buildings, and share the history of Battle Harbour. It now has the status of a National Historic District.

A guide takes visitors to the first Anglican church built on that coast, as well as the wooden stores and fishing buildings, some original homes, and the Grenfell Mission Doctor's Cottage. The Fishing Rooms demonstrate how fishing, sealing and birding were done in the past. But when the sun sets, it is those that sleep in buildings from the past and dine together on Labrador tastes who really feel the spirit of Battle Harbour. Accommodation is provided in historic houses, a small inn or the bunkhouse. Interesting conversations are shared around dining tables with the other guests. Uniquely prepared fresh local fish, moose pot pies and other meals characteristic of this area are served.

A taste of Fish and Brewis is offered as An Authentic Experience, giving visitors a unique taste of prepared dried salted fish. Just as the fishermen carried their lunches to sea in a wooden bucket, grub buckets are packed for those wishing to picnic on the rocks overlooking the sea.

To experience Battle Harbour is to taste from the sea, learn of the past and remember the men and women who worked so hard to feed themselves and others.

Lifetimes have been lived in this settlement and on the seas, and over time have changed like the winds.

COOKING THANKS

Battle Harbour, Labrador, Summer 1894

"HEY B'Y," MARY SAID to her husband Earle, " I needs you to get down to the Shop to get me some molasses that just came in on the ships. "

"Mary, won't bring in enough fish this year to cover no molasses."

Mary sighed and sat down in the rocking chair in the corner of her kitchen. Through the salt-covered window she could see all the ships in the harbour unloading their goods. Goods they could never own. Up the hill, Dr. Grenfell's new mission hospital reflected the sun. Earle sat quietly beside her, his arm in a sling after his fishing accident last week. They could never work hard enough to repay their debts to the merchants. He wouldn't be fishing for a while, so their debts to the mercantile would be too much. Both worried in silence.

"The way I've got it figured, Sister Cecilia and Sister Ada saved that arm of yers up at the hospital, and they deserve a right fine treat fer dinner," declared Mary.

That morning a fresh cod had been left on their doorstep, a generous gift from a fellow fisherman. Here at Battle Harbour, the fishermen took care of each other.

To buy a bit of molasses, they would have to bring in hundreds of fish in return. So Mary could only dream of that sweet thick taste right now.

She'd have to stick to making Fish and Brewis. She knew that Sister Cecilia loved her flummies with molasses but that would have to wait.

Earle sat quietly in the kitchen, intently watching the ships unload, and that got him to thinking. He slipped out the door quietly when Mary wasn't looking and grabbed a bowl and his old hand drill from the shed. He headed down to the docks to the shed where he had watched the barrels of molasses being unloaded. He squeezed under the wet, slimy wooden docks. Bracing his drill with his good arm, he began to make a hole in the floor above him. Nothing. He moved the drill and started another hole. He heard voices above him so he waited to drill the third hole. Finally he saw a thick brown liquid start to drip slowly, and he put the bowl under the hole to catch the molasses, while he looked for a stone to plug the hole when the bowl was full. He headed up the hill, balancing the bowl with care. A spill could give away his secret.

"Whadda ya got there?" Mary exclaimed, the cod almost slipping out of her hands when Earle handed her the bowl.

"I brung you some molasses, fresh off the ship." Earle beamed with pride.

"We ain't got no barrel of money, but that don't mean we don't know where the barrels are." And he left it at that.

Mary got to work turning the cod into fish and brewis. She had some old hard loaves already soaking for the brewis and even scrounged some old pork rinds to turn into scrunchions.

Mary would make Sister Ada's favourite–Flummies. Mary's grandmother was of Inuit background and had married a British trapper. She was sure that cooking flummies came from her grandmother's ways.

At sunset, Mary and Earle walked up the hill to the Grenville mission hospital, left their meal on the doorstep, knocked on the door and headed home.

Later the nurses opened the door to find a dinner on the stone step. They knew what a gift that meal was from their friends, Mary and Earle who worked so hard to exist.

Sister Cecilia and Sister Ada looked down the hill to the light in the window and waved their thanks.

FISH AND BREWIS

There are many ways to make this dish that was a staple of the diet of fishermen.

- 1½ to 2 lbs salted cod (any white fish)
- 5 pieces of hard bread (like hard tack of the past)
- Fat back pork
- 1-2 onions

THE NIGHT BEFORE

1. Cut salted cod in large pieces and add enough cold water to cover in pot.
2. Take about 5 pieces of hard bread and cover with water to soak.

THE NEXT DAY

3. Pour water off fish, add more cold water and bring to a boil for 5 minutes. Cool and remove bones and skin. Set aside.
4. Fry fat back pork until light brown (to make scrunchions).
5. Remove from pan and fry onions in the grease until golden brown.
6. Add water to soaked bread and bring to a boil, turn off heat and drain.
7. Add fish and onions to bread mixture.
8. Place fish and brewis on a plate and top with scrunchions and grease.

FLUMMIES

Flummies are thought to be a contribution from the Inuit women who married the British sailors. Much like "Fry Bread" of indigenous origin, Flummies were a staple and easy for the men to make out in the bush when they hunted.

- 3 cups flour
- 1½ tsp baking powder
- ½ tsp salt
- 1¼ cups warm water

MIX THE FLOUR, baking powder, salt, then pour the warm water over and mix the ingredients.

Flatten the dough into 1 cm thickness.

Using a fork make holes in the surface.

Cook in a greased frying pan for about 20 minutes.

Enjoy with molasses.

ACKNOWLEDGMENTS

MANY PEOPLE HAVE inspired and helped me put together this book.

Thanks to all those who bring bygone days alive, for the commitment and passion they show in their work at the historic sites. For putting on a wool apron and standing in front of an open-hearth fireplace so we can see what it was really like.

Thanks to those experts at the sites who helped review my material and to those who shared with me the little-known facts that added spice to the tales.

Special thanks to Shelley Denny for her short story of the Eskasoni Peoples. Also Faye Sylliboy from Eskasoni Cultural Journeys, Loretta Decker -L'Anse aux Meadows, Jane Severs – Colony of Avalon, Millie Spence – French Rooms Bread Oven, Ted Dolan – Port-Royal, Emma Doucette – Jean-Pierre Roma; Coady Slaunwhite – Fortress of Louisbourg; Greta Mossman – Ross Thomson House; Pierette D'Entremont – Le Village historique acadien de la Nouvelle-Écosse; Katherine MacLeod-Highland Village Museum; Mylene Dugas, Philippe Basque, and Marie Boudreau – Village Historique Acadien, Jenna Fitch – Kings Landing; Lynn Hayne- Sherbrooke Village; Peter Bull – Battle Harbour; Linda Little – Balmoral Grist Mill; Thea Wilson Hammond – Memory Lane Heritage Village; Juanita Peters – Africville Museum; Jason McNeil- Orwell Corner Historic Village; Adrian Morrison *Bluenose ll*; Peter Cullen- Ross Farm Museum.

Recipes have been generously shared by many of the sites and Parks Canada.

Thanks to Parks Canada for access to their material and encouragement.

Photos were contributed where credit is given, by Sherbrooke Village, Highland Village Museum, Colony of Avalon and Emily Sollows of Bluenose II and Nova Scotia Museums. All other photos were taken by the author.

A special thanks to Nancy Fischer for her patience and thorough job of editing. Thanks to Martin Gould for his creative work on the book cover. Henry Buller and Lisa Thatcher of R and R printing helped make this a book you can hold in your hands.

Appreciation to Corey Feduck for technical support.

Thanks to Olena Pylypenko who created the map.

Thanks to my husband Ranj Feduck, for his company in our travels together and his constant encouragement to complete this book.

The author acknowledges that the historic sites included in this work are located on the original territories of the many First Nations who have inhabited this land since time immemorial. I wish to pay the highest respect to their histories, traditions and continuous living cultures.

LIST OF RECIPES

PHOTO CREDITS

COLONY OF AVALON

- Credit to Colony of Avalon Foundation.

BATTLE HARBOUR

- All photos except the recipe photo–credit to Battle Harbour Historic Trust.

HIGHLAND VILLAGE

- Header photo (drone shot)–credit to Highland Village Museum.

BLUENOSE

- Photo of Bluenose sailing–credit to Emily Sollows.
- Photo of coo–credit to Nova Scotia Museum.

NOTES

NOTES

NOTES

NOTES

NOTES

NOTES